GRAB AND GO

A FOOD BUSINESS MILLIONAIRE'S SECRETS TO

ACHIEVING WHAT HE WANTS IN LIFE

JIM KIM

Translated by Hannah Pang

HARRIETT PRESS

About the Author

Born in 1964 in South Korea, Jim Seung-Ho Kim dropped out of Chung-Ang University in Seoul before migrating to the United States in 1987. He is a major shareholder in SnowFox Topco, which has eight thousand employees and more than three thousand stores across eleven countries, including the United States, United Kingdom, South Korea and France. He is also the chairman of JimKim Holdings and M3 Asset Management, president of the Korean-American Businessmen Friendship Forum, and a visiting professor at Chung-Ang University. He has coached thousands of entrepreneurs in universities and schools in South Korea, and more than eight million people have watched his YouTube lectures. He is the author of four books in Korean. He lives in Houston, Texas.

About the Translator

Hannah Pang received her BA in geography from the National University of Singapore, and her MA in international studies from Korea University in Seoul, South Korea. Her translations have been published in The Guardian. She is the founder of Harriett Press.

Originally published in Korean as *Saenggak ui pimil* by Golden Lion Books in South Korea in 2015. This edition first published in Singapore by Harriett Press, by arrangement with Golden Lion Books.

Harriett Press Pte Ltd
Telepark 5 Tampines Central 6
#03-38 Singapore 529482

Cover Design by Hannah Pang
Edited by Merl Storr
Typeset by Kerry Press Ltd
Printed and bound by Oxford Graphic Printers Pte Ltd

National Library Board, Singapore Cataloguing-in-Publication Data
Name(s): Kim, Jim Seung-Ho. | Pang, Hannah, translator.
Title: Grab and go: a food business millionaire's secrets to achieving what he wants in life / Jim Kim; translated by Hannah Pang.
Description: Singapore: Harriett Press, [2020] | Originally published in Korean as Saenggak ui pimil in 2015. | Includes bibliographical references. | Translated from Korean.
Identifier(s): OCN 1125345368 | ISBN 978-981-14-3307-8 (paperback) | ISBN 978-981-14-3897-4 (e-book)
Subject(s): LCSH: Success in business--United States. | Food industry and trade--United States. | New business enterprises--United States. | Entrepreneurship.
Classification: DDC 658.421--dc23

Our titles may be purchased in bulk for business, promotional or educational use. For more information, please email editor@harriettpress.com.

Table of Contents

Prologue

Part 1 – Success Is a Product of Habit

1 The World's Largest Bento Box Company   5

2 How to Realise Good Dreams   9

3 Two Women from France and China   18

4 The Habits of Successful Wealthy People   21

5 Lessons from Failure   26

6 There Are No Limitations   29

7 Management Lessons from a Chicken Farmer   32

8 Lessons I Only Learned at Age Fifty   44

9 Eight Similarities of Successful Entrepreneurs   47

10 How Our Company Works   50

11 I Am the Product of My Thoughts   55

12 What Others Consider Impossible   59

Part 2 – The Man Who Greets Six O'clock Twice

13 A Sense of Responsibility and Pride Even After Death   65

14 The Person Who Greets Six O'clock Twice Rules the World   72

15 The Man Who Entrusts His Wife to His Friend   75

16 The Usefulness of Studying History and Geography   78

17 Rescheduling an Appointment Is No Different from Being Late   81

18 Your Destiny Changes When You Straighten Your Back   84

19 Desk Drawers, Car Boot and Wallet   87

20 How to Make Others Quietly Detest You   90

21 Do Not Apply for Credit Cards   93

22 Resistance to Formalised Ideas   98

23 The Courage to Change Your Mind   102

24 A Conversation with Panda Express CEO Andrew Cherng   104

25 Jack Georges Bags   107

26 Why South Korean Franchises Should Enter the US Market   109

Part 3 – Sell What They Want

27 The Power of a CEO   119

28 I Am Therefore a Thinker   124

29 Travelling with American Entrepreneurs   128

30 Penetrating a $500 Million Market with Three Words   132

31 Guardhouse, Toilets, CEO's Office and Stakeholder Policy   142

32 The Right-Behind-Person Strategy   147

33 Frontier Uprising or City Revolution   150

34 What to Look Out for When Your Business Grows   155

35 The Significance of the Fruit Trees in Our Headquarters Garden   163

36 Twelve Signs of a Failing Business   166

37 Seven Reasons Why a Kind CEO Fails   169

38 The Hardest Thing About People Management   171

39 Change the Rules   174

40 How to Increase Customers Tenfold   177

41 Selecting the Best Talents   180

42 How to Make Employees Work Independently   184

Part 4 – The Miracle of Repeating Your Goals a Hundred Times a Day for a Hundred Days

43 The Problem with Immoderate Kindness   191

44 Work Till You No Longer Work for Money   194

45 Gathering Powerful People Around the World   199

46 Self-Determination   204

47 Trade or Business   207

48 The Economics of Footing the Bill   211

49 Praise for Indolence   213

50 Finding Order in Chaos   216

51 Give to Receive   219

52 Weaknesses Become Strengths When Disclosed   221

53 Thirteen Differences Between the Successful and the
Hugely Successful   225

Part 5 – Let's Be Kind and Faithful, But Shrewd and Indolent

54 The Mistakes and Megalomania of Intelligent People   231

55 Money Is a Person   233

56 The Differences Between Frugality and Miserliness   235

57 Heaven Is Here   237

58 No One Has Got Rich by Diversifying Investments   239

59 Horoscopes, Blood Types and Multilevel Marketing   242

60 The Worst Wife, the Worst Employee   244

61 My Reasons for Making Money   248

62 A CEO Should Be Healthy   251

63 Bad Customers   253

64 How Extravagant Should Wealthy People Be?   255

65 The Seemingly Irrelevant But Essential Matters in Business   258

66 If You Wish to Gain the Other Party's Respect   261

67 Growing at Forty, Stopping at Forty   264

68 The Courage to Admit Ignorance   266

69 Statistics Are Lies   269

Bibliography   272

Epilogue   273

Prologue

I have three sons. All three were born in the United States and are more proficient in English than Korean. At home I speak Korean, but my sons converse in English. Having everyday conversations with my sons isn't a problem, but it isn't enough for them to thoroughly comprehend their parents' language.

My children are amazed to see my books displayed in bookshops whenever they visit South Korea. I was worried that my children – who longed to be the first people to read my books – were ultimately unable to fully comprehend them. But one day I got news that an English edition of this book was in the pipeline, and I was ecstatic. People think that this book contains stories about me, and about the business of an entrepreneur who has achieved the American dream. But the truth is: this isn't a book about my business. It is a collection of essays that illustrate, through entrepreneurial experience, how one person has realised desires that many people have.

I grew up in the East, and worked in the West after becoming an adult. I was a poor immigrant who became a person that travels the world for business. Since then, I have met countless successful people around the world, but there is no difference between East and West in how people realise their dreams. I still think that the methods for realising and managing our desires are simpler, and come from smaller places, than we think. My business has expanded several times over since this book was first published in Korean, but I still live according to the same methods and attitudes.

I hope this book will be of help, however little, to my children, and to young people in the West, in realising their dreams as they delve into the ideas with which a young immigrant – who spoke no English, and had no academic degrees or capital – built his life. I conclude with the hope that you will remember me as a thought engineer who skilfully applied the secrets of his own thinking to realise his dreams, rather than as a successful entrepreneur.

Part 1
Success Is a Product of Habit

If a wealthy person knows what poverty is, they know the beginning and end of wealth. And if they understand Pablo Picasso's words 'I'd like to live as a poor man with lots of money', they will never be ruined. I deeply respect the experience that my failures have gifted me. And I am proud of making an impressive comeback after the age of forty because of the lessons I gained from my failures. There is nothing to boast about if I hadn't failed. This is because I don't know when I will fail. There is therefore absolutely no reason to be ashamed of our failures. We should rather worry about not failing. If we draw lessons from failures, any failure can help us succeed.

1

The World's Largest Bento Box Company

The words 'The World's Largest Bento Box Company' are inscribed in large font on a black board pasted to a window east of our office. But if you look a little closer, 'Here' appears in small font at the top, and 'Was Launched Too' at the bottom. At first it seems as if only 'The World's Largest Bento Box Company' is written there, but when both the small and large texts are read together, they suggest that we have become the world's largest bento box company, and that this is where other businesses will be conceived too. Having started out with a bento box business, our company has been expanding into the food distribution and food manufacturing sectors as well as growing as a general food company.

Words have power the moment they become sound and emerge from our lips. The first chapter in the Gospel of John illustrates this principle well. Words are power. Sound gives form and meaning to words through language, so words have power the moment they are conveyed to someone or when they reach our ears. This power refers to a real, physical power. Words course through a person's thoughts before they appear to us. And when they are visible as written words, their power is demonstrated whenever we read them.

The best way to amplify the power of words is always to write them down. People who believe in the power of written words turn every desire into a symbol and carry it around with them, calling it a talisman. The superstitious element of talismans is exaggerated, but there is no significant difference between a talisman and the words 'Get into SNU'[1] inscribed above a desk.

I am someone who believes in the power of words. I believe that the power of words that are spoken once doesn't dissipate until they are forgotten. To constantly endow words with power and ensure this power doesn't dissipate, I handwrite words within a frame and then display them, or I construct suitable images and turn them into a poster. This is the first thing I do to actualise a new personal goal or a new company goal. I have achieved innumerable goals by always doing this.

This was also what I did when we purchased our current office building. Early one morning – days after we had viewed the building for sale, and before we had financed the purchase – I stopped by surreptitiously, took a picture, added the words 'Our Future Office Building', enlarged them, and put it on display. We are now working at lovely desks in that stylish building, some of us wearing ties. It is inconceivable that only a few years ago our employees were working six to a desk in a warehouse building. Without taking out any loans, we bought the newest building we could find. It's surrounded by sturdy fences and comes with a lake, a vegetable field of a few thousand square feet, a garden that could fit an upmarket coffee shop, the most luxurious office furniture and desks, an abundance of cabinets, and a warehouse that can load sixty cargo containers. This all started with a picture taken surreptitiously one morning.

The product of my experience is that I can achieve anything by constructing an environment that constantly stimulates my thinking. Some time ago, I created a long email password: 300storesweeklysales1milliondollars. The reason was that after starting this business, I aspired to achieve weekly sales

---

1   Translator's note: SNU is Seoul National University. It is one of the most prestigious universities in South Korea.

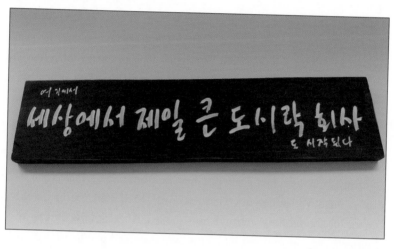

여 기에서

세상에서 제일 큰 도시락 회사

도 시작 됬다

'I am someone who believes in the power of words. I believe that the power of words that are spoken once doesn't dissipate until they are forgotten. To constantly endow words with power and ensure this power doesn't dissipate, I handwrite words within a frame and then display them, or I construct suitable images and turn them into a poster.'

of $1 million from three hundred stores. By repeating these words multiple times a day, every day, I was influenced by their power.

As a result, I never forgot what our company goals were. However, I changed my password in 2012. I had achieved those goals and was ready to set new ones. My new goals were three thousand stores and annual sales of $1 billion. Shortly after setting these goals, I received requests to open hundreds of stores in Colorado, California, Washington, Oregon and Alaska, and there was a queue of requests to open stores in most of America's prominent supermarkets. If these requests continue, our annual sales could surpass $1 billion. I might need to retain a long password for just a few more years to reach our goals of three thousand stores and annual sales of $1 billion. Our company, which achieved annual sales of $5 million in 2013 thanks to a lengthy password, is now expecting not tenfold but several hundredfold growth.

I have always liked farming. When someone asks what I do in the company, I tell them I set goals, put them on posters or in frames, and then display them. When they ask what I *really* do, I tell them I farm and drive the tractor around the company's back garden. Although the CEO's work is unseen, our company has been anticipating several hundredfold growth during the past few years. If people ask me the secret to this, I tell them about the trivial methods that help me focus constantly on my goals by engraving them on my mind through repetition. And then I always feel that they just plainly don't believe me, because they invariably think there must be other secret methods. It's exasperating how often I must repeat this to those who haven't experienced how great the power of visible goals can be.

2

How to Realise Good Dreams

Would you believe me if I told you that an egg was worth $100 million?

6 November 2009 was the day before my meeting with Charles Woods at the Kroger Co.'s headquarters in Ohio.

When I woke up, I vividly recalled the dream I had had the night before. I was stretching out my stiff back after working vigorously on a farm when three hunting men approached from afar. 'What are they doing on someone else's farm without permission?' I wondered, and I asked if they were having fun, but they said they weren't having much fun and shrugged their shoulders. However, behind them came a fox whose neck was chained. The fox, which was clearly chasing after the hunters, looked terrified.

They entrusted the fox to me and then went on their way. As I warily embraced the fierce-looking fox, its wounds – the cause of which was unknown to me – healed. The fox's face became slightly distorted because of the new scars. All the while, it folded its front legs obediently and remained in my embrace. It was wonderful to embrace a wild animal so freely, and it was pitiable too, so I was still embracing it gently when I woke up.

My meeting with Charles concluded half with expectation and half with apprehension. Charles is the manager of the deli division at Kroger, which owns more than two thousand five hundred stores. He wanted to select four companies to manage more than eight hundred bento box stores in supermarkets across the entire United States. These bento box stores were currently being run by eighteen companies. While deciding which four companies to select, he met with us to learn more about the size and structure of our company.

If we were selected out of the eighteen companies as one of the final four, we could feast on a twenty-five percent market share in America. Conversely, if we were eliminated, we could lose seventy percent of our sales. I thought we were better than any competitor in the southern United States, or in the whole country. But the nature of our business meant that there were plenty of variables, and I couldn't feel entirely confident unless Charles completely ruled out any form of pressure or misinformation.

'Yes. Crisis is opportunity,' I thought. I was mulling over how to resolve this problem after returning from the meeting when I recalled my dream from the night before. I then designed a project for our company to seize this opportunity and take another leap forward. I christened this project 'Operation Capture Red Fox'. The reason was that I interpreted the fox entrusted to me by the hunters in the dream as their bento box business.

First I sat at my desk and searched the Internet for pictures. I found a picture of four men with a small wooden box before them, posing as if they were about to swing the poles they held in their hands; next I found a suitable picture of a fox. Using CorelDRAW, I combined the two pictures into a passably nice image that resembled a film poster. I titled it 'Operation Capture Red Fox' and added the words 'Cincinnati Film Festival 2010 Best Picture Award', complete with laurel leaves around the words. Since it was a film, I started off in the lower part of the poster with Jim Kim as director, and I randomly wrote other roles next to our employees' names, so it was undoubtedly a film poster.

I printed the poster and pasted it onto every door in the office. Then I started to do what I have always done whenever I want to be sure of succeeding at something. As I had done this exactly four times in my life, and had succeeded remarkably on all four occasions, I had no doubt that I would succeed stunningly on this fifth occasion.

What I did was to repeat my goals a hundred times a day, for a hundred days. My goals were clear and specific: three hundred stores across the United States, and annual sales of $50 million with weekly sales of $1 million. I also included the goal of operating more than fifty premium stores already being operated by Kroger. We had barely got our hands on just one of those stores, but was anything impossible?

On 22 February it was a hundred days since I started repeating these three goals. It was the 102nd day since I had started, to be exact: I had skipped two days. Meanwhile, what had transpired? On the ninety-sixth day, a company that had treated us coldly when we had called them during the early days of our business contacted us; and on the same day, a company in Atlanta, Georgia, which hadn't scheduled a meeting with us despite our knocking on their door for the past three years, reached out to us. And, finally, on the 104th day, we heard directly from Kroger's vice-president.

This was the process by which vice-president Jeff Burt contacted us. One day, we heard that Kroger's CEO David Dillon would be visiting a store in Houston, Texas, with sixteen regional presidents and key executives. We had a store there. Our employees and I acted swiftly. We first searched the Internet for the names and pictures of Kroger executives and produced pamphlets to introduce our company; then we set up a food-tasting booth at the front of our store and waited for them to pass by.

As soon as the CEO and regional presidents arrived, our employees verified their physical descriptions by phone, and then steadfastly introduced the company and handed out pamphlets to every one of them. Some regional presidents recognised that our products were superior and showed a keen interest. One of them was Bruce Lucia, president of the Atlanta office, which we had been badgering for the past three years. But the vice-president of the company's deli division, Burt, didn't show up in the end. If we had got hold

'What I did was to repeat my goals a hundred times a day, for a hundred days. My goals were clear and specific: three hundred stores across the United States, and annual sales of $50 million with weekly sales of $1 million.'

of Burt, opening three hundred stores would have been a walk in the park. We didn't give up on the executives who responded that Burt was in charge every time we introduced our company, and appealed to each one of them.

We also presented Dillon with an appreciation plaque, which we had pestered a souvenir manufacturer into producing in a day. The plaque was inscribed with words of gratitude from all our employees and store owners for working together in Kroger stores, written in their respective native languages. When Dillon received the plaque, he said he would carry it with him personally, and was as delighted as a child.

*

I was building a Korean-style sauna on my farm when I received a call from an employee to inform me that Burt had contacted us. I said, 'Really? I must finish building this sauna, so schedule an appointment two weeks from now…' On 15 March, I flew to Cincinnati, Ohio, for the meeting. It was the 121st day since my goals had been set. On the morning of the meeting, our company's vice-president, who was also attending, shared a dream he had had that morning.

He said it was a dream in which he had received a tray of eggs, and he had sorted them because there were rotten and fresh eggs. He asked me if that was a good dream. Instead of answering, I pulled from my bag a blue egg that I had brought from my farm. 'What kind of egg is this?' asked a surprised employee seated with us. I said, 'We will know later!'

Our meeting with Burt, at a quiet Japanese restaurant on a hill in downtown Cincinnati, went well. We agreed on a comprehensive overhaul of Kroger's bento box business, and we decided that our company would take the lead on this endeavour. We were persuasive and could give clear answers to all of Burt's questions and objectives, because before the meeting we had already conducted several rounds of mock negotiations to identify the questions that Burt would have to ask, and we had thoroughly put together our answers to them. When we were close to concluding our agreement, I cautiously pulled the blue egg from my coat.

'I brought this from my farm yesterday morning. It's fresh for a few days. However, it might become rotten if you leave it as it is, or it could grow into a chick if you placed it in an incubator. The bento box business resembles a newly laid egg. It seems like it's coping well now, but it might become rotten if we don't manage it now, or we could grow it into a giant business. If we want to grow our business into a colossal business, let's sign this egg. I will take the egg back to Houston and place it in an incubator. And if a chick is born, I shall name it Kroger.'

The vice-president gladly signed the egg, followed by the other executives seated with them, Charles and his boss Ann Reed. We decided there and then to transform the whole of America's grab-and-go bento box market, starting the following month with the state of Virginia. It was clear that if things got going, our company's accomplishments over the past five years would increase yearly, and we could achieve three hundred stores and weekly sales of $1 million by as early as the end of the year.

'I have no idea what you guys did in Houston, but our executives placed your business cards on my desk the day after they got back. I was in a position where I had to make a call,' Burt said. As our meeting ended, Burt smiled and added, 'I asked Charles, and he said he felt the best about your company among the sixteen companies.'

It didn't even take four months for all of this to transpire. Before placing the egg in an incubator when I got back to Houston, I took a picture of it and produced another poster. I wrote the words 'Another Hundred Million Dollar Blue Egg' under the egg.

I amended our company's goals. To annual sales of $100 million. When external visitors to our company saw the posters pasted in various places, they asked if we produced movies too.

It looks Fresh but only for the few Days
It can spoil if We left it alone
or
Becomes the Chick which lays another 100 million eggs.

DO YOU SEE WHAT I SEE

Another **100 Million**
Blue egg

'The vice-president gladly signed the egg, followed by the other executives seated with them, Charles and his boss Ann Reed. We decided there and then to transform the whole of America's grab-and-go bento box market, starting the following month with the state of Virginia.'

'On 19 March 2011, we achieved weekly sales of $484,431. I promptly ordered five cars from a BMW dealer. Each employee who had been with me from the outset received a car.'

We simply looked at the words 'Mission Completed', which had been added to the top of the 'Operation Capture Red Fox' poster, and beamed.

In 2007, I promised to buy every employee a BMW if we achieved weekly sales of $480,769 (based on annual sales of $25 million). On 19 March 2011, we achieved weekly sales of $484,431. I promptly ordered five cars from a BMW dealer. Each employee who had been with me from the outset received a car. Our sales had been growing by around twenty-five percent yearly, but we recorded an increase of more than forty percent in 2010 and expected an increase of as much as hundred percent in the following year. This was made possible because our $100 million egg had hatched, and we had started to expand across Virginia, North Carolina, South Carolina, West Virginia, Utah, Arizona and so on.

Subsequently, we unlocked the markets in neighbouring states including Ohio, and other states such as California and Colorado, becoming a national company in both name and deed. The success of that one-year period left a mark as large as the total sales achieved since our company's inception. A little bento box company, which had sprung up from a southern Texan city crowded with cowboys, had expanded within two or three years to the point where it was eyeing the number one position in the industry in America. I was delighted to see BMWs thronging the company's car park. I was delighted by the fact that my thoughts had become reality.

3

Two Women from France and China

One day, during a time when my business was still taking shape, two women visited me at almost the same time, one from France and one from China. Among the countless people I got to know through my business, most of the men wanted to learn how they could ultimately gain a good franchise store; but intriguingly, these two women badgered me into teaching them the way I did business. All I knew about them was they had read my book *The Kimbap CEO*[2] and had come searching for me halfway across the world without a definite plan.

To conclude the two women's month-long training at our Houston headquarters, I sent them back to China and France. Most men came looking for me because they wanted to run a restaurant, but I was surprised and impressed that these two women had visited me to acquire my entire business management system, and therefore I coached them as conscientiously as if they were my younger sisters. Hee-Seon returned to China and set up stores in supermarkets near Beijing, and Kelly reached an agreement with France's largest supermarket and started to open new stores. If there was a difference between them, it was that one wanted to learn about business while the other wanted to learn about my life. Hee-Seon, who wanted to learn about

---

2   Seung-Ho Kim, *Kimbap paneun CEO* [The Kimbap CEO] (Seoul: Hwanggeumsaja, 2015).

business, grew sick of convoluted tax regulations after opening ten stores in China, where the franchise system hadn't yet fully developed; Kelly, who wanted to learn about my life, started to spread our stores across the whole of Europe at a rapid rate.

I had been contacted by countless individuals. They were people who took up the gauntlet to realise clear goals: Eun-Hye, a female university student who wished to become an entrepreneur; Seung-Geun, who couldn't abandon his food business dreams despite having a respectable job; Seong-Eun, who said she yearned to be like Kelly, and who learned the ropes for a month before flying to Europe; Ji-Yeon Baek, who aimed to found a social enterprise while working in a lovely office; Yeong-Ah Kim, who desired to succeed in the fruit and vegetable business and had visited the venue of my lectures without a definite plan; Soo-Ro Kim, who ran a *bingsoo* shop in Hongik University in Seoul; and many others, including Hyeon-Jeong, who came all the way to the United States without a clear plan, and who caught me off guard by saying she wanted to work for us.

Surprisingly, many people find it daunting to make bold requests of socially successful people. But those who seek out successful people, challenge themselves and face snags in this manner will discover the next opportunity. I don't think that all the young people who have come to me are successful. But I have no doubt that countless successful individuals have arisen from this group of people who have made such efforts.

Kelly imitated me by writing out a list of goals. And, one by one, she began to achieve them. The list covered everything from business to personal life. She meticulously imagined everything, from the looks of her future husband to her future child, a house and yacht that she wanted, and so on. A few years passed, and Kelly realised all her goals. After a few failed businesses and unsuccessful relationships in France, she proudly made an impressive comeback. Kelly married a great Frenchman. They had a charming baby girl, Mia. They asked me to give her a Korean name, so I named her Ji-Yoo.

Kelly went beyond France and began to establish stores across the whole of Europe, building a company whose scale of business was second only to ours in the United States.

I learned that it isn't easy for conceited people to succeed. Often, when we decide to operate a business and then look around us carefully, we see that things that are worth doing have already been done, and we don't know what we should do. Many people have read my book *The Kimbap CEO*, but why do some perceive opportunities in the book, while others are content merely to read it? Those who seek to learn and challenge themselves glimpse a light even in minuscule opportunities, and possess the curiosity and passion not to simply pass that light by. This passion creates the door to success.

'Brother! I did well in imitating you, but I left out one item when I was writing my wish list,' said Kelly, with whom I had formed a personal relationship. This was after an annual company meeting in Houston had ended, and she pulled me into a corner, glancing at her husband who was standing in another.

'What more do you need?' I asked.

'I… had put the height and looks of my future husband on my wish list, but I left out the part about a fine head of hair,' she said.

I wanted to smack Kelly on the back, but I held back patiently and simply smiled, because there were a lot of people around us.

4

The Habits of Successful Wealthy People

Successful people come from a background where they can't help but succeed. This background doesn't include their parents' assets, usually described as 'backing'. It's unclear whether this background is shaped by education or acquired independently. But most successful individuals share some surprising similarities. Thomas Corley investigated these similarities in his book *Rich Habits*.[3] The commonest habit of successful individuals is reading. More than eighty-eight percent enjoy reading more than thirty minutes a day. Conversely, only two percent of poor individuals enjoy reading. Most economy class passengers on long-distance flights enjoy watching movies, but business class passengers either work or read thick books.

Successful individuals always have a book close at hand. Their books are commonly seen in all kinds of places: bags, office desks, bedsides, cars and so on. There are times when they are filled with dismay after they finish reading a book. The dismay of having lived their lives thus far without having known what they have just read in the book. There is also the horror of realising how many experts there are on earth. They consider it good fortune to have survived without this knowledge and wisdom, so they can't possibly stop learning. This is the reason why they always have a book in their hands.

---

3   Thomas Corley, *Rich Habits: The Daily Success Habits of Wealthy Individuals* (Minneapolis: Langdon Street Press, 2010).

That is why eighty-six percent of successful individuals believe in the power of lifelong learning. It's a colossal difference compared with five percent of poor individuals. While eighty-six percent of wealthy people like books, only twenty-six percent of poor people feel the same. There is a ninefold difference (eighty-one percent versus nine percent) in the number of people who jot down their daily tasks and, interestingly, a categorical difference in the number of people who regularly exercise more than four times a week (seventy-four percent versus one percent). This is because wealthy individuals recognise that our minds and bodies are organically connected.

Furthermore, there is a fourfold disparity in the numbers of people who set specific goals (eighty percent versus twelve percent) and who record their goals (sixty-seven percent versus seventeen percent). If we consider the time when people get out of bed, which shows whether individuals spend their mornings effectively, there are three and a half times more wealthy people who rise three hours before leaving for work. These everyday habits of successful people converge to form the fundamental background of success. The lives of entrepreneur friends around me are no different. Entrepreneurs in South Korea too are no different.

There is a franchise CEO programme at the Yonsei University Graduate School of Business in Seoul that brings together and trains South Korea's franchise entrepreneurs. Two years ago, I completed this programme while commuting weekly between South Korea and the United States for close to four months. During that time I met numerous entrepreneurs, both veteran and rising.

Most of them were self-made entrepreneurs. Although their origins, educational levels and journeys differed, most had similar habits. They were full of curiosity, they constantly asked themselves if there was anything they could learn from others, they were good at listening, and their goals were clear. They knew what they wanted to do. We had late-night discussions and drinking sessions on the days we attended training together; but they showed excellent stamina, participating in meetings early the next morning, feeling refreshed, and in some cases even having worked out in the meantime. If there was a slight difference between South Korean and American entrepreneurs, it was the high percentage of South Korean entrepreneurs who made use of the Internet, sundry lectures and connections because they were bored with acquiring information from books.

However, whether in South Korea or the United States, successful wealthy individuals have three things in common. First, their perception of liabilities is markedly different. They respond swiftly to the impact of a one percent difference in bank interest rates and a 0.25 percent fluctuation in the central bank's interest rate, and take steps to address their liabilities. But poor individuals have no idea what the interest rates for credit cards or personal bank loans are. They don't even know that they can negotiate the interest rates for the loans they are currently repaying, or the interest rates of the diverse financial products introduced by banks.

Second, the way they perceive problems is different. Typically, when a problem occurs in a company, an employee writes a report about it. But the initial report contains the opinions of that employee. Most people assess a situation based on the initial report. However, if the initial report is biased or distorted for some reason, all assessments will be erroneous from the outset. This is the commonest scenario in which a problem snowballs into a bigger one. For this reason, successful individuals strive to be objective about the initial report. They master the habit of freely questioning the established views found in news items or social phenomena, and of thinking independently about the causes and impacts of those phenomena.

The third similarity is that they are more interested in an incident's positive rather than negative aspects. They are interested in silly ideas, and look for the good in an incident when it occurs. They don't lose heart or give up easily.

It's almost impossible to defeat a positive person. A person who eventually discovers even a minuscule possibility believes in that possibility and waits with anticipation. The words of a hopeful person don't contain anger or exasperation. There is no power in conversations or thoughts mixed with anger or exasperation. Successful individuals therefore always look bright, and don't go around looking gloomy.

Success is the product of long-time habits. And every decision we make as a result of these habits converges to form our reality. When success comes unexpectedly one morning, like a win in the lottery, to a person who lacks these good habits, it will disappear before long. I hope young women remember when they choose their future husbands that with these good habits he can succeed independently.

Customers who were drawn to the Asian chefs clad in long aprons and unique caps looked on with great interest as the chefs skilfully made, sliced and packaged *kimbap*. The cooking process had become a show. Customers who wanted to learn to make *kimbap* were dressed in long aprons and caps and then led inside the kitchen. They bought the *kimbap* they had made themselves. The audience applauded when they sliced carrots and fashioned butterflies out of them, and when they selected oranges and moulded flowers out of them. It felt as if a meek, lovely girl were performing a song shyly but superbly.

Extract from *The Kimbap CEO*

5

Lessons from Failure

I have been operating businesses since I was young. I have operated numerous big and small businesses, from small stores to fairly large companies. I failed multiple times before my current business; but looking back, from each failure I learned what I should or shouldn't do now.

I first opened a blanket store after coming to America. The price of quilts in America was more than ten times more than in South Korea. I stared at the profit margin that capitalised on this fact. But there were countless American consumers who wished to buy certain colours of blankets, curtains, bed covers and pillows as a set, and in those days South Korea didn't have the concept of buying in sets. As I didn't understand consumer culture, there was nothing consumers would buy even if they visited my store. Consequently, I wound up a business that I had started without even conducting basic market research. I learned that the market comes first.

When I founded multiple newspaper companies, I didn't recognise the problems that could arise when partnering with individuals who didn't set clear boundaries between shareholders and executives. Some shareholders thought of the executives as their employees. Subsequently, I made it a rule that I would not do business with individuals who had no experience of working in partnerships. When I was operating a securities and futures company, I learned the principle that past achievements don't guarantee future profits. To think otherwise is akin to believing a fortune teller who says a person can know their own future by knowing their past. I was ashamed of having risked everything I had without knowing this principle. However, I learned that a person's asset portfolio or a company's fate in the face of the massive flow of financial organisations is like a candle in the wind. I knew at that time that the purpose of investing was to make money, but I had absolutely no idea that investments could become the assets of individuals who had already made money. Since then, I have acquired a macroscopic view of investing. I lost a great deal of money, but I was fortunate to have picked up the skills for managing wealth.

When I operated a Korean grocery store, I learned how tedious it could be to run a business with a closed market structure. As a result, I started to keep an eye on the industry instead of the business. When I was running a computer-assembling company with a business partner, I realised that, regardless of the size of my stake in the company, I was drawn to things I was ignorant of. The reason was that I had no interest in a business where I couldn't learn, even if I made a great deal of money.

The failure of my organic food store wasn't exactly my fault. But I learned that in the face of uncontrollable events – such as the sudden business fluctuations caused by the 9/11 attacks, or long-term roadworks carried out by a new government – large businesses that can't raise the capital required to pull through such events will collapse more easily than small businesses. I also learned that a kind boss isn't a good boss, and the horror of interest rates.

Who will help self-made bosses learn these lessons, and where can they learn them? Back then, I felt pangs of heartache each time things fell through; but looking back now, I see that each failure has become a huge lesson and an asset. If I hadn't learned even one of these lessons, I might sink again if I were to meet another obstacle in my current business.

If a wealthy person knows what poverty is, they know the beginning and end of wealth. And if they understand Pablo Picasso's words 'I'd like to live as a poor man with lots of money', they will never be ruined. I deeply respect the experience that my failures have gifted me. And I am proud of making an impressive comeback after the age of forty because of the lessons I gained from my failures. There is nothing to boast about if I hadn't failed. This is because I don't know when I will fail. There is therefore absolutely no reason to be ashamed of our failures. We should rather worry about not failing. If we draw lessons from failures, any failure can help us succeed. I hope you aren't afraid. Success abides by a very simple principle: constantly challenge yourself, even if you are constantly failing. Then someday you will meet your successful self.

6

There Are No Limitations

William is a friend of mine who migrated from Argentina to America when he was young. He is a film director and philosopher. He lives in a unique world of his own, and he constantly dreams of capturing the meaning of life and achieving commercial success through his films. His dreams are big. I believe William will shake up the American film industry someday. This is because I believe he can do it, and I believe in what he believes in.

One day, while we were in the car, we realised we both had the same concern. It was our despair over how hard it was to coach and help our subordinates, or people around us who were conscious of their personal limitations, to understand that there are no limitations. Perhaps William had heard countless disapproving remarks. It isn't easy to produce films in Houston that will outperform those from Hollywood. And few of the individuals who assist him with his films have had the experience of surmounting this limitation. His team therefore constantly set up limitations and say that it's risky, they feel uneasy, be careful, it isn't going to work, and then they confine themselves within their own self-made limitations and think they are right. They have no idea that there are no limitations unless they set them. They think instead that setting limitations is a way of understanding how the world works.

I am always the first to tire of battling such negative thoughts when setting news goals with our employees or carrying out a new project. When we had ten stores and were dreaming of three hundred, there were people who mocked us, and others who were thrilled. When we looked at our three hundred stores and spoke of three thousand, there were people who admitted defeat, and others whose hearts raced. When I said we could become a conglomerate by selling bento boxes, there were people who turned their backs on us, and others who pondered our going public.

I wasn't conscious of any limitations. I am always ecstatic about new plans. But there are always people who don't believe they will overcome the next limitation, even though they made progress by smashing a previous one. They resemble disciples who have abandoned their teacher even though they have seen miracles and studied under him or her every day. Books on positivity have long ranked among the bestsellers in bookshops. A product that sells well for a long time is a good product. Positive thoughts refuse to place limitations on us. They imagine us overcoming our limitations. Our minds can't tell whether our imaginings are real or fiction. Therefore, our own imagination works with the imaginations of all the people around us to become reality. Some people will mock these bold claims, and others will be as astounded as if they had been kicked in the backside. Then the mockers will disappear, and the astounded ones will achieve their dreams.

The reason for teaching others by using metaphors is simple. It is so that only those who will understand can understand. William and I have no energy left to explain at more length than we are doing now, to people who are conscious of their own limitations or even impose limitations on others, that there are no limitations. That said, I believe this little book might change someone's life.

The intensity of desire is the measure of success. A strong desire thus promises more definite achievements. I can share with you a simple physical formula to achieve reasonable and logical desires. The formula is as follows:

$$F = K \frac{q_1 q_1}{r^2} = \frac{1}{4\pi\varepsilon} \frac{q_1 q_1}{r^2} = 9 \times 109 \frac{q_1 q_1}{r^2}$$

This formula is hard to comprehend, so this is how I will explain, in one simple sentence, to those who have given up trying to understand: verbalise your desires a hundred times a day for a hundred days.

Extract from *The Kimbap CEO*

7

Management Lessons from a Chicken Farmer

When I was young, the yellow chicks that were sold in front of my school tended to die. It was rumoured that the seller was peddling chicks with fatal diseases. But having personally raised chicks on a weekend farm as a hobby, I felt sorry for the seller, who had been absurdly misunderstood. When I bought chicks for the first time, I presumed it would be awfully difficult to raise them because of my childhood memories, but the majority flourished when I paid attention to them and just controlled the temperature. Chicks only grow well if the temperature is close to forty degrees Celsius, but most of the chicks that fell into the hands of children when I was young died of hypothermia.

I usually buy chicks in America by mail order. Nowadays I order from the Internet as well, but elderly folks who wish to raise a few chicks in their back garden as a hobby generally order from a catalogue. There is a poultry farm with a hatchery in a small country town called Cameron, two hours from Houston. The poultry farm starts to offer all breeds of chick for sale from February every year.

I gave them a call. Like a member of the nouveau riche who enters a Chinese restaurant and haughtily says 'Give me one of everything on the menu', I said, 'Please send me ten chicks of each breed.' Then they replied,

'We have one hundred and fifty breeds. Is that all right?' Startled, I ordered only ten breeds. It turned out the hatchery was one of the largest specialist poultry farms in America, with several hundred thousand chicks hatching yearly.

More than twenty days later, a postman brought the chicks in a parcel with holes in it. I was surprised that the postman was carrying live animals with him, and that they could be delivered anywhere in America using such packaging. I learned that the delivery was possible because chicks can survive on the nutrients in their bodies, even if they don't eat or drink, for three days after they are born.

As directed by the poultry farm, I hung a mini-heater in a paper box and adjusted the temperature to thirty-seven degrees Celsius. I placed food and a water bottle that contained some sugar in the box. One week later the chicks leaped over the box, and two weeks later their wing feathers appeared as they began to grow. In the second week I gradually reduced the temperature, and on the third week I removed the heater. Excluding the chicks that friends with their own gardens had purloined as pets for their children, three or four at a time, I moved all the remaining live chicks to a coop that had been prepared on my farm beforehand.

But that was when the problem started. Mountain animals near the farm knew that dinner was served, right in their territory. I had already named two guard dogs, Ho-Dong and Soon, and assigned them the role of protectors while raising them with the chicks, but the wild dogs in the vicinity attacked the chicken coop before the guard dogs had grown. They didn't just devour one or two; they killed more than twenty chicks for sport, and fled.

The harm caused by the wild dogs lessened when the farm's perimeter fence was raised higher, but now wildcats that could leap over the fence found their way in. In less than two months, there were fewer than ten chicks left. I pridefully ordered four hundred more chicks. Three hundred of them died. Unable to stay on the farm all day, I had to devise all sorts of ideas to protect the chicks from wild animals. This time I gradually raised the height of the chicken coop's door from knee level to chest level, to keep out the mountain animals that leaped over the fence while the chickens were asleep.

Soon the chickens had been trained to come and go from the meadow by jumping through the coop's windows. Consequently, the harm to the chickens started to diminish. As soon as Ho-Dong and Soon had grown to weights of more than fifty kilos and begun to patrol the coop, the mountain animals and wild dogs conceded defeat and disappeared. Throughout the night, Ho-Dong, who thought of the chickens as his family, would patrol the coop and bark at the slightest sound. He would therefore doze during the day to make up for lost sleep while the chickens pecked his ears and nose. Unlike Ho-Dong, who was relatively benevolent towards wild boars and deers, the bitch Soon spent the days chasing large beasts. They were an impressive pair of dogs, suitable for poultry farming, and they had divided their roles between day and night.

But our struggle hadn't ended. Every other night there was a strange occurrence in which one or two chickens were completely taken apart, leaving only the bones. The dogs stood guard in front of the coop's door, and no badgers or wildcats passed by. Initially I suspected it was either Ho-Dong or Soon. But they were cleared of suspicion after the same thing happened in the chicken coop when the door was locked. I was sorry for needlessly having shoved the dead chickens into their faces to coerce a confession.

It turned out the culprits were mice. Mice tinier than your thumb. During the day, the mice would burrow into the earth under the water bucket or sack and hide there; then, when night came, they would gnaw away the anuses of the sleeping chickens. The chickens, which couldn't do anything in the dark, would collapse and die in the meadow or coop in the morning. Other chickens, no longer considering the dead remains to be their comrades, ate them up and left only the bones. This ongoing game of attack and defence continued in this way between nature and me as I raised the chickens.

I flipped through the newspaper and looked for anyone who was giving away a cat for free. I received two three-week-old kittens from a Mexican who was in a hurry to move elsewhere. As soon as the cats, which loved to play during the night, started looking for mice, there were no more dead chickens. It seemed nature had given in to my defence. One day, as I pondered how nature might attack next time around, I noticed something odd about the chickens playing in the field. I couldn't see any cocks. It turned out that when the wild dogs, badgers and wildcats had come to eat the chickens, the already small number of cocks had attacked first, to protect the hens, and had died. With a brood of hens and no cocks, I would have to find someone who raised chickens on a farm like I did and purchase a few more cocks from them.

I looked on Craigslist and phoned a farm that sold cocks. I had absolutely no idea then that meeting the woman at her small farm to buy three or four cocks would radically change my concept and ideas about managing my farm. This meeting also deeply influenced a later change in my business trajectory and goals.

*

Amanda Powell was a former primary schoolteacher. As soon as she learned of my intention to run my farm organically, she spoke effusively about her respect for Albert Howard and explained that she was a follower of J. I. Rodale. To Amanda, agriculture was more philosophy than science. I followed her and looked around her farm. It consisted of forty acres of grassland and three acres of vegetable fields. There were about twenty cows, a herd of goats, several hundred chickens, and three or four horses. When I asked what she produced primarily, Amanda said she grew grass. I wondered if growing grass was too small-scale to make a living, but she explained, 'Grass is, in other words, meat.' She explained that she was a farmer who grew grass and turned it into meat. She said it as if it wasn't so complex.

'The livestock on our farm does as it pleases,' said Amanda.

Amanda understood grass as an ingredient that formed the foundation of her agricultural produce. Her work on the farm addressed the issue of symbiosis and aided the cyclical movement of every plant and animal. She had divided her farm into a few sections and fenced them off. First, she would send the cows and goats into section one to graze. A few days later, she would send the chickens into the section, using a mobile chicken coop. The chickens fed on the larvae and insects in the cow dung, and the scattered chicken dung served as nitrogenous fertiliser. The top part of the grass that remained after the cows had eaten it – which the chickens liked to eat – would be appropriately cut. The chickens consumed insects and grass and laid the highest-quality eggs, with yolks that were almost bright pink.

The cows, goats and chickens would then be moved to section two, and section one would be off-limits for a month. Meanwhile, the grass would grow more abundantly than before. This was a story of how the land suffered absolutely no harm, instead becoming more and more abundant through this production process. Pointing at the buds that had sprouted from seeds sown where the goats' little hoofs had passed, Amanda said, 'There is nothing in nature that isn't linked to another thing. We must think of the earth, plants, animals and humans as one gigantic circle as we run our farms.'

Then I realised that her farm was one of the countless family farms in America similar to Joel Salatin's Polyface Farm in Virginia.

'Do you know how appalling current organic farming practices are, compared with what most people think organic products are? Organic farming doesn't stop with talk about organic farming. It should be used to balance organic relationships in the whole production process. We wander far from the original purpose of organic farming if we only use organic matter as fertilisers and not as pesticides. If consumers are interested only in price, won't producers be interested only in output? However, if consumers are also interested in product quality and the value of life, organic farming is the wisest response.

'Organic farming is a term we can never surrender to conglomerates, but we have already been dispossessed of a great deal by them. You will have seen labels like "free-range chicken" or "stress-free chicken" among the organic chickens sold in supermarkets. The "free-range chicken" label applies to chicks that are confined for six weeks after they are born, in the name of protecting them from "unknown threats", and subsequently a small side door connected to the chicken coop is kept open for thirty minutes a day for two weeks, in the name of giving the chicks the "right to go outside". That is the law. Do you know the meat is from chickens slaughtered in their eighth week after they were confined? Organic eggs aren't particularly different. They come from chickens that merely ingest organic feed and are bred as a group in an always-cramped chicken coop.

'When you visit an organic grocery store, you can see instant food products that are labelled as one hundred percent organic products. But you can never be assured that they are organic when you check their contents. The government has already yielded to conglomerates' lobbying and allowed such products to be labelled organic. If this continues, we may need to discard the word "organic", whose meaning has already been corrupted. Some of us have started to use the words "beyond organic" for our farming style or our products.'

The words 'beyond organic' soon sounded like a magic spell to me. They accorded a fundamental value to the purpose of farming. They were also consistent with Laozi's maxim of *sangseonyaksoo*.[4] Amanda gave me some profound homework to do as I strived to operate my company as she did, 'independently'. I had raised chickens to produce eggs. But after

---

4   Translator's note: *Sangseonyaksoo* (상선약수/上善若水) is a maxim from the *Dao De Jing*. It means that the best virtue resembles water, which benefits all creatures but doesn't compete for gain.

hearing what Amanda had said, I had a stronger desire to produce eggs and simultaneously respect nature.

That day I paid Amanda $50 for five Ameraucana and Golden Buff cocks. After releasing the cocks on the farm, I decided not to abide by the economic principles commonly used in farming. I was determined, because I wanted to be like Amanda: a conductor that helped my farm achieve harmony in nature. I longed to become a real farmer, not a part-time one. The cocks, which had been thrown into a crowd of hens, found their place.

The costliest processes in agricultural production are usually purchasing fertilisers or feed, and packaging and distributing the finished products. I resolved to eradicate these costs. Thus, I developed the laziest method of poultry farming by secretly implementing the methods I had learned from Amanda. It sounds grandiose, but it's a method our grandmothers traditionally used. It's the method of not feeding the livestock but releasing them into the pasture as Amanda did. But I couldn't place the chickens in a mobile coop and move them every few days, as happened on Amanda's farm. I still had to report to work in the city during the week to manage my actual business.

First, as a trial, I divided the land into one acre for every two hundred chickens, also including the two dogs. This area of grassland was sufficient for the chickens. I simply ignored the contagious diseases or harmful insects most feared by the agricultural industry, and I chose not to use medication as a preventive measure. For a lazy person like me, this was a truly attractive method.

Most far-reaching calamities occur when livestock is raised in a group in a cramped space, but I took comfort that this would never happen to chickens that frolicked all day in amply spacious chicken coops and a meadow. I also heard that if a few chickens do die, it's nature's censor weeding out the weak to keep the survivors healthier and healthier. In only a few months, the chickens were laying more than a hundred eggs daily. The chickens leave for the field as soon as day breaks, then return to the coop and sit on straw nests when it's time to lay their eggs. Several hens brood around twenty eggs each. Many mother hens are already embracing their chicks. Ho-Dong and Soon too have produced seven puppies, and I don't stop the hugely curious hens from looking in on the litter.

There are equal numbers of blue, brown, dark brown and white eggs, and they are of numerous sizes, from tiny ones like quail eggs laid by Silkie chickens, to baseball-sized ones with double yolks. The dark-green pasture outside the chicken coop is exceedingly invigorating. Sometimes I let the goats in, just to reduce the height of the grass. Now, if I simply help to refill the 1,600-litre water bucket connected to the chicken coop once a month, and Ho-Dong and Soon's fodder buckets once a fortnight, I can get several hundred eggs a week. There are leftover eggs even after I share them generously with family and friends. I have started to surpass my initial goal of producing at least enough eggs for my family's consumption.

Nature and the dogs raise the chickens on my behalf. Like Amanda, I obtain top-notch organic products using extremely inexpensive labour, without even hurting the farmland.

*

The 'beyond organic' method of farming that I learned from Amanda also influenced my current business. I had started in business for survival. Honestly, as a young man I hadn't had the easy kind of adulthood where I might champion business as a noble cause. I was the eldest son, and it was gruelling to settle as an immigrant with my ageing parents. When people think of American immigrants, they somehow think of idyllic stories about individuals moving to America with a few hundred dollars jingling in their pockets and then achieving the American dream. But the reality for me was no different from the lives of South-East Asian youths living in South Korea now.

It was utterly depressing to know little English, to have ridiculously inadequate capital and a degree that mainstream society didn't recognise, to be treated warily and secretly despised as a foreigner. As I couldn't secure a professional job, my whole family had to survive by working their fingers to the bone. At that time it was my dream to spend a day with my family, comfortably, not just on Sundays but Christmas and New Year too.

However, as soon as I had the ability to provide for my elderly parents and children, and my number of employees was increasing and I had to sustain thousands of lives through my business, I needed a reason for us to work together. I strived belatedly to find a reason for doing business. Not every employee had joined the company to survive, as I had. It's apparent that everyone in a company has different directions in life, which are as numerous as the employees. For one employee our business might be a great company that can't be found elsewhere, but for another it's simply a place to work; for one we might be a great company where they do their utmost to realise their life goals, but for another we might simply be a company that is close to home.

For first-generation immigrants like me, there is no better reason than to survive in a foreign country; but for Americans, or for second- and third-generation immigrants who are proficient in English and well educated, that same reason is as antiquated as an elderly Korean who drones on about hardships during the Korean War.

Fortunately, as I wrestled with this problem and studied the mission statements of numerous companies, I observed many instances where companies had devised their missions retrospectively as the number of company members grew, and had cultivated their company culture collectively as they expanded. The company owner's everyday philosophy usually becomes the mission of the business, but it wasn't easy to turn my philosophical interests – which border on idleness – into a company culture. I loathed philosophical things and, with or without them, it didn't seem as if we would be bonded as we are by collaboration and honesty. After I had wrestled with this problem for countless days and months, something struck me unexpectedly. Amanda's 'beyond organic' method of farming was the answer.

Ultimately, the primitive goal for you and me to live well together was the fundamental reason why we were in business. To put it plainly, it became our business goal to 'do what is good for everyone'. If a business is good for our company members, customers, partners and society, it's a business worth doing. However, if it isn't good for just one of those four parties, it isn't good for us either. Is our business good for our executives and employees? If yes, we can increase work productivity and profits if we enhance employees' job security by raising their pay and improving their welfare. This is ultimately good for our executives and employees.

It's good to use good raw materials and set reasonable prices for customers. It's good to pay our partners and support our subcontractors' financial wherewithal by paying them promptly, regardless of industry practices. Conversely, when we pay contract employees exploitative wages, covertly use poor-quality products, bully subcontractors by requesting goods at cost price, and cheat on our taxes, someone will make a profit, but it won't be good for everyone, because those on the other side will be sustaining losses.

I believe a company can grow substantially even while doing what is good for everyone. We have done that so far and will continue to do so. Over the last decade, we have never been sued by any of our store owners, who number more than a hundred. We are an extremely exceptional case in the United States compared with our competitors of similar size, which sigh at the number of lawsuits that pile up yearly. Our company hasn't had any lawsuits or intensified disputes with our employees. No argument with a customer has ever culminated in a lawsuit. That a company with more than

'I envision an organic method of doing business, just as there is an organic method of farming. I hope that the 'beyond organic' business perspective will spread, instead of the situation where all executives focus only on one-sided interests.'

one thousand two hundred stores in America and globally has never gone to court since its inception is something worth boasting about.

The concept of 'work that is good for everyone' will impact our entire business in the future. Organically, we grow together by doing what is useful for one another. I envision an organic method of doing business, just as there is an organic method of farming. I hope that the 'beyond organic' business perspective will spread, instead of the situation where all executives focus only on one-sided interests.

8

Lessons I Only Learned at Age Fifty

My youngest child brings an iPad over and shows me a number. It clearly says twenty-seven years, two months, four days and six hours. When I stare at him as if asking what it means, my son explains it's the number that indicates his father's remaining time on earth, and it has been generated by a program that calculates a person's remaining lifetime. I see. The intelligent computer knows that I have fewer days ahead than the days I have lived. No wonder my life insurance premium has been getting ridiculously expensive.

I did feel perplexed that half of my life had passed by in a flash, but I also wished to pass on to those who will come after me the experiences that age has given me. This is driven by the same logic as visiting a place and hoping to share bits of information that will guide others who pass by that place later. I want to chronicle these lessons especially for a younger generation – those in their forties. We often hear others say 'If I were only ten years younger'. I contemplated what I would or would not do if I could go back to ten years ago. The following are lessons that a fifty-year-old would like to pass on to those in their forties.

1. Maintain the right posture. Stick your buttocks close to the chair and straighten your shoulders. The right posture will help you live comfortably in old age.

2. Never be afraid of making mistakes. Failure has two benefits. You don't make the same mistakes again, and you are given the opportunity to trial a different method.

3. Go to bed early, and rise early. From the past to the present, early risers have always set the rules and enjoyed success.

4. Never stop hoping. It's hard for you now, and it won't get easier later, but it's only the belief that you won't stay like this forever that will always keep you going.

5. Do not envy youth. To constantly envy someone else's age is itself a form of behaviour inappropriate for your age. Today is the day of your life when you will look the youngest.

6. Do not cling to your children. Do not prioritise your children once they are in primary school. First tend, pay attention to and have fun with your life partner.

7. Even if you lie to others, at least do not lie to yourself. Quit saying 'When is there time to exercise?', 'I have no plans to get married', 'Looks like it's genetic'.

8. Be kind. Do not talk too much, stop any immoral behaviour right now, offer your seat, respect the opposite sex, do not grumble over food. And never lose your temper. Poor habits that aren't discarded after forty will stay with you till the day you die.

From the standpoint of someone who has lived for more than a decade after forty, I can think of countless apparently insignificant but necessary lessons. When the time comes, everyone will deeply feel the usefulness of these lessons. If I had adopted and applied these lessons a decade ago, my life would certainly have been steadier and more beautiful. But I know from history that humans don't learn from history.

Since prehistoric times, we have always felt regretful after learning too late how to honour our parents. Nowadays politicians are considered inane, and young people are said to be becoming more impudent. These are remarks we have heard since Roman times. We know that history repeats itself, but humans repeatedly don't learn from history. Therefore, even if I write at length these lessons from a life mentor, people won't be all that eager to read them before the age of fifty. Only after fifty will they wish they had heeded, and will they harp on these lessons as I do. I hope at least one person will look at my mistakes and not repeat them.

9

Eight Similarities of Successful Entrepreneurs

I have had the opportunity to meet myriad types of entrepreneurs from diverse industries. Although those who have built businesses on a certain scale have very diverse management styles, they share several similarities. They all seem to have reached the top on their own. Here I chronicle the lessons I have learned from them.

1. They are undaunted by criticism or praise. They are neither discouraged when criticised nor thrilled when praised. They know the criticisms will someday cease, and fervent supporters will suddenly appear in the front row on the opposing side.

2. They work smart rather than hard. Hard workers can't rival those who like their work, and those who like their work are no match for those who enjoy their work. But even those who enjoy their work have no way of competing with those who work smart.

3. They are punctilious about small things, but indifferent to big incidents. Their indifference to big incidents is actually a façade. They know instinctively that the stems and branches will fall should the roots falter. Thus, when big incidents occur, they often tackle them by staying calm, as if indifferent, and they focus meticulously on the small things, as they could snowball into big incidents.

4. They loathe and like simultaneously. Only those who have become leaders can comprehend this. Successful entrepreneurs have people or hobbies they loathe but like. And they never let others know.

5. They don't pretend to know what they don't know. There is a difference between trade and business. Trade is when entrepreneurs train each employee themselves because they know best about every task. However, a business truly begins when employees are more proficient than their boss in every task. These bosses aren't ashamed of not knowing certain tasks, and they transform each employee into an expert in the company by encouraging those who excel in those tasks.

6. They are prudent with small sums of money and spend big sums freely. They recognise that it's possible to be frugal with most small sums because they are spent through inertia, but big sums are spent on necessary things.

7. They enjoy days off. They enjoy without fretting. They know full well that by being absorbed in work all the time they can make a small business successful, but not build a big business. They know to enjoy days off and rest, because they know that life isn't about living in expectation of future rewards – that the present too is life. And they know that this will eventually culminate in bigger success.

8. They don't seek to destroy competitors. On the contrary, competitors are partners. Even if they destroy one competitor, others will show up, so they simply seek to do better than their competitors, and stop trying to destroy others and have it all.

Of course, these similarities don't apply perfectly to everyone. However, people who live the lives of executives know full well that they are imperfect, and they don't attempt to do everything alone. The strongest person in the world isn't someone who is in a high position or wealthy. The strongest person is someone who has countless people by their side who will come to their aid, who has numerous friends who don't wish to see them fall, and who has won the greatest number of hearts. I am certain that successful entrepreneurs are not where they are by good fortune alone.

10

How Our Company Works

Every company has a unique corporate culture. I have developed a list of guidelines to preserve and expand our corporate culture. These guidelines encapsulate all that I have written over a long period about what is necessary while performing my role as a CEO. Some of these guidelines I noted down after I heard them elsewhere and they resonated with me, but most I wrote to address my own needs. The nine guidelines are as follows:

1. You know what the company is doing now, and the company knows what you are doing.
2. First report the facts, then present your opinions later.
3. If you wish to complain, propose an alternative.
4. There is a deadline for everything, and work submitted after a deadline won't be praised, no matter how well it has been done.
5. It isn't necessary to love one another. But respect one another, and keep your emotions out of work.
6. All work is carried out through a system.
7. If you undertake work that you alone know and can do, you will always be doing only that or will fall behind.
8. If there is a problem, there is also always a solution. If there is no solution, alter the problem.
9. Start every task meticulously, then continue simply.

Here are the rationales behind each of these nine guidelines:

1. **You know what the company is doing now, and the company knows what you are doing.** I appropriated the first guideline after chancing upon a broadcast programme. These words had briefly appeared during a scene in which JYP Entertainment's Jin-Yeong Park was coaching Korean pop stars. Many employees are often oblivious of the paramount task the company is currently facing. Executives also don't communicate what the major current tasks are. However, employees who embrace this guideline will be promoted, and bosses who understand it well will obtain actual results.

2. **First report the facts, then present your opinions later.** The second guideline is designed to routinise factual report writing that doesn't incorporate personal opinions. When reporting an incident, employees often write reports that incorporate personal opinions like 'Something bad has happened', 'The other party wants to pick a fight', 'It seems they are up to something' and so on. But employees should assess an incident with their superiors. If personal judgements take precedence, the report might be distorted, and superiors might make distorted decisions based on the distorted report. A problem can be properly assessed only if opinions are stated after a situation has first been explained factually.

3. **If you wish to complain, propose an alternative.** The third guideline was constructed to stave off grumblers in the company. All grumblers do is grumble. By grumbling they show that they are smarter and wiser. This promotes division in the company, devitalises the atmosphere, and in severe cases creates sympathisers. Employees who simply grumble without proposing an alternative should be dismissed.

4. **There is a deadline for everything, and work submitted after a deadline won't be praised, no matter how well it has been done.**

It doesn't suffice to stress this fourth guideline just twice or thrice. Superiors repeat the mistake of giving orders without specifying deadlines, and subordinates long to be praised for their work, even if they only worked on it when the deadline was fast approaching or had even passed. I consider overdue work as work not done, just as a tardy apology isn't considered an apology.

5. **It isn't necessary to love one another. But respect one another, and keep your emotions out of work.** The fifth guideline acknowledges actual limitations in human relationships, and seeks to eradicate the adverse impact of such limitations on work. It's great if employees cherish and love one another. However, just as this isn't how society works, there are bound to be people we like or dislike in a company, and we can't dismiss someone whenever that happens. If someone obstructs work simply out of jealousy or envy, or simply stands by when this happens, the entire organisation will become diseased. In the realm of work we should be respected, even if we are unable to love one another.

6. **All work is carried out through a system.** This guideline isn't needed for small organisations with three or four employees. But organisations with more than ten employees must work through a system. A system refers to established rules and an organisation's ability to develop and uphold reasonable rules. A company with no system morphs into a different company whenever its members change. Every time this happens, the company squanders enormous quantities of time and resources to adapt to a new organisational culture. Founding members are dismissed, or are branded as exceedingly loyal but incompetent individuals when they overlook or are unable to uphold the new system. Founding members who are unable to grasp this will eventually be discarded once they are no longer useful.

7. **If you undertake work that you alone know and can do, you will always be doing only that or will fall behind.** This is how people behave if they fear being dismissed or are led by a desire to secure personal influence in a company. From the company executives' standpoint, it may be a pity to dismiss these people, but one can never promote them. Those who are unable to coach their juniors, or who are ignorant of the rule of progressing alongside their colleagues, must do only what they know and can. They will be the first to be dismissed when their job is no longer needed in the company.

8. **If there is a problem, there is also always a solution. If there is no solution, alter the problem.** The most exasperating employee is someone who conveys what they have heard. When they say 'The other person says they won't do it' or 'This is the only solution', it doesn't show that they have the will to solve the problem; it conveys their desire not to solve the problem. A problem is something to be solved, and we urgently need a culture that seeks out countless solutions that can eradicate problems. When there is an increasing number of employees who are unconscious of the need to challenge themselves, the company will surely fall behind.

9. **Start every task meticulously, then continue simply.** One day, I saw an elderly woman knitting on a park bench. The tangled skein in the basket by her side was oscillating between two bamboo sticks and morphing into a scarf. I observed how complexity was transformed into simplicity through a certain process. Simplicity is neither imprudence nor juvenility. In all we do, we must be truly meticulous at the outset. And straighten it out until our work becomes the simplest. Then we can always preserve the details. A company's strength and potential lie in the details. But the nature of details is fastidious, inconvenient and complex. The continual preservation of details incurs enormous stress and costs. We need the know-how

to simplify details and to sustain the efficiency produced by the simplification of details. The scarf looked like a strip of thick fabric when seen from afar. However, when I looked more closely, each stitch in the complexity was exquisitely connected. Simplicity, after all, is the perfection of detail.

Here are four specific pieces of behavioural know-how to support these nine guidelines:

1. Report completed work. Prepare an interim report on tasks that require more than a day to complete.

2. Start meetings at times that end with a prime number (for instance, 10.01 am, 9.07 am, 11.23 am), keep meetings under thirty minutes, and hold afternoon meetings only in an emergency.

3. Do not use email for work that has to be done via phone, do not use the phone for work that has to be done face-to-face, and do not meet face-to-face for work that can be done via email.

4. Respect the scheduled time for leaving work, and do not contact employees who have left work about work.

All these guidelines and pieces of know-how are based on an organic company whose 'work is good for everyone'.

11

I Am the Product of My Thoughts

If I were to ask you to choose between the power to know the future and the power to create the future, which would you choose? Well, the answer to this question has already been determined. We don't have the power to know the future, but we can create the future. Humans are curious about the future. Everyone is. Although there is no evidence that we can know the future by knowing our past, we listen intently to fortune tellers and even take them seriously.

The past leaves traces on us. It leaves numerous traces such as the backs of our hands, our facial expressions, our attire, the way we move our shoulders, the way we walk and so on. Fortune tellers can learn a great deal about us with just this amount of information. But we can only follow and infer from these traces, because no one knows the future.

The fortunate thing is we can create the future even though we have no knowledge of it. This is the inherent power of humans who have life and thought. Everything that has life possesses the power to flow, however briefly, against the world's physical tides while it is alive. This reasoning is illustrated in the fact that all non-living things move along in the direction of the water, but living fish can swim upwards against the tide. And when we continue to harbour determined thoughts about life, we will gain the power to constantly swim against and emerge from the tide. When living things think, they create the future by going against nature. And, in a broad sense, this is a natural phenomenon.

Humans have no knowledge of the future but are born with the power to create it. The fascinating thing is that this power is given to the person who believes it, but a person who doesn't believe is convinced that they don't possess this power. There is an apple in a box. The one who believes and opens the box will receive the apple. The one who thinks there is no apple will receive none, just as they expected, because they won't even open the box.

The Buddha left us these words: 'I am the product of my thoughts.' My existence is the product of what I have thought over the years. If I change my thoughts now, I will change myself and my future.

People often diet to get in shape. But a person's body is the product of their daily habits. When we change our daily habits, we change our bodies too. We should change our daily habits, not diet, to get in shape. We can attain a far more wonderful figure just by cultivating the right eating habits and postures. And only by changing our habits can we maintain our figure without experiencing a yo-yo effect.

The same is true of us. Everything we have now is the product of our thoughts. We may never have wished for these things, but they are the product of our thoughts – even negative thoughts. This is because our thoughts are unable to comprehend negativity and positivity. There is a lady who said she would never return to her former rotund self, then superimposed her own face onto the body of a heavily built woman and uploaded the picture to her phone's lock screen. In this case there is a huge possibility that she might inadvertently turn out like the photo, because her thoughts can't discern between negativity and positivity. That is why a positive attitude has a positive impact on our lives.

Now look around where you are seated. If you are at home, consider the tables, chairs, blankets, computers and cup of coffee, which all came into the world because of someone's imagination. Open the window. Everything that unfolds before your eyes – buildings, roads, cars – originated from someone's imagination. You are now living in other people's imaginations. Because they imagined these things before you did. Previously they imagined not just things but morals, ethical constraints, social regulations, laws, concepts, opinions and political agendas, and then they confined you within them. This is possible because you never imagined them, and someone else imagined them beforehand. These people have mastered the power to transform imagination into reality using a tool called thought. They use this power to economically and politically govern and exploit countless people who are unable to think or imagine. They are creating their future on their own. As their thoughts grow stronger and more tenacious, their opponents become more powerless and even lose the freedom to think or imagine, ending their lives as accessories in the imaginations of others.

There is only one way out. We must acquire the power to think independently. We shouldn't read a news article and think 'I see.' There is an intention and objective behind every written thing on earth. You must think independently to find out what they are. Even when we come across a book by a renowned writer, we shouldn't succumb to its authority; we should examine it and learn to digest the author's writing. If you are learning from a teacher and you gradually become dependent on them, they aren't a proper teacher. A true teacher is someone who teaches their students to stand on their own two feet and walk on their own.

We also ought to discard the prejudice that the road taken by the majority is the right road. Dictatorships have come to the fore by relying on the power of this prejudice. Religions are especially perilous. Many religions nowadays drive their believers to demolish independent thinking. Religions have no value as religions when they don't respect free will. This is because I am an object, not a human, when I have no assurance of free will. Why should I respect a God who treats me as an object? This will never happen if God loves humankind, so we should be exceptionally wary of religious leaders who preach such teachings. All religious teachings that demand unconditional faith and renounce doubt are no longer religions.

I am me.
I am the product of my thoughts.
I can live the way I want.
I can create the future I want.
This is because I have the free will to read this essay and think independently, whether to agree or disagree with it.

12

What Others Consider Impossible

Everyone has a secret dream in their hearts. For some people only traces of these dreams remain, while others are kept awake every night by their impassioned hearts. We hide these dreams in a corner of our hearts, like a garment that is neither worn nor discarded, and we lead our lives. Some people put their dreams in a corner because reality is too harsh for them to work towards realising those dreams. And some think they have simply missed the opportunity after wavering and hesitating. Some have given up prematurely after suffering a couple of defeats. That said, these dreams still wait to be summoned one day from somewhere deep within our hearts, and are now just holding the fort. They are holding out pitifully, like mudfish trapped in a drying puddle.

The person who knows me best in this world, after all, is me. But people stop me by saying 'You aren't suitable for this job', 'Know the subject', 'Don't do it. You will get into unnecessary trouble', 'You don't have the experience or ability to do that'. In fact, those who stop me are people who haven't even attempted the work I am trying to do. They denigrate and hinder me from realising my potential – which I too haven't seen – on the basis that they raised me, that we have grown up together, that we are friends, that they know me well.

But let's ponder for a moment. Is there anyone among those who have left their mark in this world, whether big or small, who have succeeded and accomplished their dreams, who hasn't heard negative prejudiced opinions about themselves? Who believed that the notes Fyodor Dostoyevsky wrote on his palms in the prison camp would be published as a book? How about Henry Ford, who realised his dream – which even his father mocked – a century ago, when there were no proper roads? How much opposition did Oprah Winfrey overcome, being born a black woman in the South where racial discrimination was rampant, before becoming the most respected woman in America?

A few years ago, I saw a scene in a TV programme where the South Korean comedian Bong-Won Lee was teased. Every business he started had foundered, so he was getting advice like 'Please listen to your friends next time' and 'Listen to the people around you and decide if you should or shouldn't run a business'.

I recall that Lee's friends, who appeared on the programme, felt sorry for his recurring failures and offered advice that implied that he, like them, shouldn't start a business. But I am fully on Lee's side. How can those who haven't even failed advise those who have tried and failed? If you haven't failed, you haven't tried. People learn and triumph over every single mistake made by ninety percent of the population through nine repeated failures. And they get back on their feet with the last successful attempt. None of Lee's friends had experienced failures as diverse as Lee's. Who should advise whom?

One of the most exhilarating achievements in life is to achieve what others said was impossible. Don't you want to defy the prejudices and unfavourable circumstances around you, to proudly stand against the world and overcome them, just once?

All these things – the phones in our hands, cars, computers, enormous aeroplanes, electricity, electromagnetic waves, TVs – were once difficult to comprehend, even in imagination, but someone defeated untold opposition and brought each one to fruition.

Who said you couldn't be a CEO?

Who mocked when you said you would someday own that building?

Who reminded you of your age when you said you would get a doctoral degree?

What fellow told you two to break up because you were incompatible?

Who said you wouldn't walk again?

If your dreams seem unimaginably herculean, then work unimaginably hard. You just need to be confident that you will work unimaginably hard. If you have never heard someone tell you that you are mad, you have never risked your life and challenged yourself. Kites fall in a fair wind. They rise with the headwind. You must know that when the headwind blows while you are working on your dream, you are being given the opportunity to rise higher. I hope this year you will rise and face all the thronging headwinds to achieve what others said was impossible in your life.

Reader's Digest

When there is something I want or wish to achieve, I always imagine it first. I won my wife by imagining us together, and I arrived in America only after imagining it and repeating it countless times in my heart. When I saw a company that I liked, I stopped by their car park every morning before going to work, and I repeated a hundred times in my mind every day that 'I am going to buy that company'. Four months later, without paying a single cent, I acquired that company, which was worth $500,000, and I clinched a business deal worth $4 million using the same method. Even now, I have written down in my notebook more than twenty financial goals and numerous dreams that I wish to achieve. I write my dreams on one side of a piece of paper the size of a business card, and I include pictures that visualise these goals on the other side.

Extract from *The Kimbap CEO*

Part 2

The Man Who Greets Six O'clock Twice

Since the beginning of human history, no self-made individuals have slept in and still succeeded, and no one has slept in and still preserved the power and riches inherited from their parents. No dictator or rapacious entrepreneur has ignored the morning sun and still maintained their lifestyle. The sun raises everything on the land to its feet and makes it flourish. Those who drive, exercise and stretch themselves when the morning sun rises ascend the first step to success. These individuals have succeeded and ruled the world so far and will continue to do so in the future. If you consider yourself diligent, you must ask yourself if you have ever risen in the morning and greeted the sun when things went wrong at work and when you were physically unfit.

13

A Sense of Responsibility and Pride Even After Death

When Rick met me for the first time, he immediately spoke to me in an aggressive tone.

'Hey, young friend. Who on earth built this fence? If you build it this way, it will collapse in less than three years. I am not saying I want this job, but the fence will be rock solid for twenty years if I do the job, so just let me do it.'

I had bought a farm in the vicinity, about thirty minutes from home, and was about to embark on my role as a novice farmer during weekends. If not for Rick's suggestion that I entrust him with the fence work, I would have taken him for a local gangster who had come to pick a fight because I hadn't abided by the neighbourhood's peculiar method of fence-building.

Rick was a white man over sixty, and his family had been farming for generations. But he no longer farmed and had been constructing fences for more than twenty years. The only equipment he had was a twelve-inch spiral drill hanging on his small tractor, and a hammer in his hands. A native in the neighbourhood, he lived on Hosak Road, which had the same name as his father's family. Until then I had no idea that he monopolised all the fence construction in the neighbourhood. Moreover, I didn't know how talented he was at driving stakes into the ground and encircling them with wire netting. But fence construction was indeed not something anyone could do. The front gate of my farm was 1,697 feet long, but I couldn't even cover a hundred feet in two days. Having exhausted myself in just two days, I wondered if I had other urgent matters to attend to, and was looking for excuses to delay the fence construction.

'A friend of mine came and built this. Is there anything wrong with it?'

Disheartened by his request for work – which he had expressed vehemently, as if he were furious – I couldn't tell him I had built the fence, so I used a friend as an excuse. 'Young friend. Come and look at this,' he said as he pulled me to one end of the fence and pointed with his finger. As a matter of fact, I knew roughly what I had done wrong, even before he spoke a word. Then he changed direction again and pointed at a neighbour's farm fence that he had built. The fence he had built was adjusted to the thickness of the wooden stakes, and the stakes were arranged side by side across several hundred metres without one centimetre of misalignment, but my fence didn't have even three stakes in a straight row.

'It isn't just that. This Japanese cedar has been chemically conditioned so that it doesn't rot in the rain, but if we cut the wood with a chainsaw to modify its height at the top, rainwater will enter the cedar, its interior will rot in two years, and it will crumble when we touch it.'

He then tapped his finger on the fence made of felled Japanese cedar and said, 'Besides, if we turn the top part of the cedar and hammer it into the ground, it will tilt more easily. And we must pull the wire netting more firmly than this to prevent the fence from falling over or crumbling when animals rub against it. I heard you want to raise goats, but the gaps at the bottom of the wire netting are too wide. On days when the goats fancy the grass on the opposite side of the fence, either the goats' horns will get entangled in the barbed wire and they will die, or your fence will die. I offer my help because your fence looks so pathetic, and not because I want this job, so just let me do it.'

Before he heard my response, he returned to his car, tapped at his calculator and said, 'I charge $3.25 per foot for this kind of fence. The price of rebar has been rising day by day recently, so it will be impossible to get this price if you delay any longer.' He then folded his hands and leaned against his car with an expression that asked when he could start. I no longer had the power to decide. I could do it at half the cost, but I reckoned it would be better to trust Rick than to do this every three years. And I had a great excuse to stop the onerous job of driving stakes into the ground.

'Can you start right away?' I pleaded, now that my predicament had changed.

'I can't do it this week, but I will complete it by next Thursday,' he said.

A week sufficed to complete the job, but when Tuesday came and Rick didn't show up, I started to be confused as to whether he had said he would complete or begin the job on Thursday. However, on Wednesday morning, Rick showed up with a black assistant, Affney, who cursed incessantly. First, they dug the ground and planted two strong twelve-inch-thick wooden stakes, one at each opposite end where the front gate would be. Then they hammered two more wooden stakes of the same size at both ends, one after another, at intervals of six feet, before diagonally winding thick wire multiple times around the two sets of three wooden stakes to tighten them. Labour that demanded strength from every joint of Affney's body was lubricated by uninhibited expletives. Rick loaded all the equipment onto the tractor and drove to the end of the fence. Affney, who couldn't get a seat on the tractor, followed behind and cursed at every step. After hammering the wooden stakes at the end of the fence in the same way, Rick took a can of cola from the icebox, without offering me any, and finished it in a gulp. Affney took a can of warm beer from his bag and drank it.

Once the pillars on both ends had been completed, they connected the single-lined barbed wire that joined both pillars. As soon as they had pulled the barbed wire across using the tractor, an orderly boundary line appeared.

Rick followed the line and, using the spiral drill hanging on the tractor, started to dig holes in the ground that would hold the wooden stakes. Into every hole he dug, Affney poured a bucketload of expletives before thrusting in the wooden stakes. He tamped down the ground firmly with a hammer and erected wooden pillars everywhere. The wooden pillars, which had been cursed generously, were firmly instilled with military discipline, like soldiers who had completed basic military training, standing abreast in a line without an inch of error. By sunset Rick's six cans of cola and Affney's twelve cans of beer were all emptied. Rick's face was covered with perspiration, and Affney was reeling, but I could see that a hundred and seventy wooden stakes clad in wire netting were standing in a line with their backs to the setting sun. These two men had accomplished in a day what I would have taken more than a month to complete. While drinking beer and tottering.

*

The farm looked dignified, and its territory was defined once the fence formed a boundary. I was elated, thinking that now whoever wanted to enter this land had to obtain my permission. But the Pyrenean Mountain dogs that I had raised disagreed. It seemed even 4.6 million square feet of space wasn't enough for dogs that were determined to pursue the bitches whose scent drifted in from several kilometres outside the farm. They repeatedly dug the ground under the fence, coming and going every one or two days. I couldn't keep constant watch over the dogs, which had been negligent in guarding the chickens and goats, so, using a bulldozer, I began to heave up the soil under the fence to cover the ground.

But it wasn't easy covering the ground under the fence and driving around properly with only two months of unlicensed bulldozing experience. The fence gave way when a couple of stakes somehow tilted slightly. I tried to fix it by winding wire netting in various places, but I still loathed the way it looked, and it was shoddy. Rick dashed towards me; perhaps he had seen my lone endeavours from afar when he was passing. He had seen that a corner of the fence he had built was in bad shape. That was why he had stopped his car and flown into a rage.

'Hey, young friend! If you don't leave my fence alone next time, I won't sit back and do nothing,' he said.

Rick had clearly pointed at my fence and called it his. I initially thought he had said that because he felt sorry for the ruined fence, which he had built with such commitment, but looking at his face, I knew that wasn't the case. He looked like he wanted to tear down the fence he had built and give me my money back if I didn't stop right away. Overwhelmed by his fervour, I turned the bulldozer around and pulled over. Once I had stepped back, Rick continued in a somewhat gentler tone; perhaps he felt embarrassed.

'Hey. Young friend! It's true that this land is yours, and this fence was built with your money, but this fence is mine. Any fence I build should always stand upright, and it shouldn't tilt or break its wire netting, even when a new year comes around. Because I built it. That fence will be standing tall even after I die. I didn't tell you the specifics, but though everyone else uses eight-foot wooden stakes, I bought ten-foot wooden stakes and dug as deep as your height before planting them. I also used wire netting that was two millimetres thicker than what other people use, and I wound it around the wire joints two times more than other people do. You don't know the difference, but the people in this neighbourhood can recognise the fences I have built, even though there are no marks on them. You too will soon find out which are the fences I built when you drive around at fifty miles per hour.'

It took some time before I realised what he said was true. As Rick had said, all the fences he built remain upright and straight even now, after five years have passed. The value of Rick's fences stands out as time passes. In the end, I could only acknowledge that the fence on my farm wasn't mine but Rick's.

'It took some time before I realised what he said was true. As Rick had said, all the fences he built remain upright and straight even now, after five years have passed. The value of Rick's fences stands out as time passes. In the end, I could only acknowledge that the fence on my farm wasn't mine but Rick's.'

As a CEO, I have employed countless individuals in my life, but Rick was the first person who wanted to maintain his sense of responsibility and pride in his work even after death. This is an attitude to life that appears only when we respect both ourselves while we are alive and the people we will leave behind when we are dead. Therefore, who do we look up to, if not to people like him?

14

The Person Who Greets Six O'clock Twice
Rules the World

My niece had a boyfriend. Curious, I asked her what he was like.

'Does he read books?'

'I don't think so, uncle!'

'Is he punctual?'

'Yes. Initially he was, but nowadays…'

She trailed off at the end of her sentence. Finally, I asked another question.

'Is he an early riser?'

'Guess not…'

She was like a daughter to me, so, in a fatherly tone, I immediately said, 'Dump him!'

General Motors CEO Daniel Akerson rises at 4.30 a.m. Walt Disney Company CEO Robert Iger rises at 4.30 a.m. Starbucks CEO Howard Schultz rises at 4.30 a.m. Apple CEO Tim Cook rises at 4.30 a.m. too. Twitter co-founder Jack Dorsey rises at 5.30 a.m. Tory Burch, CEO of her eponymous American fashion label, and Virgin Group chairman Richard Branson both rise at 5.45 a.m.

The world is ruled by people who greet six o'clock twice a day. There are two six o'clocks in a day. Six o'clock in the morning, and six o'clock in the evening. People who don't get out of bed when the sun rises can never comprehend the magnificent energy gained by those who rule under the sun throughout the day. Whoever wishes to succeed and stay healthy should master the habit of rising early to greet the dawn and begin the day with the sun. Any riches and successes that are achieved without seeing the sun will someday pass like the wind.

Since the beginning of human history, no self-made individuals have slept in and still succeeded, and no one has slept in and still preserved the power and riches inherited from their parents. No dictator or rapacious entrepreneur has ignored the morning sun and still maintained their lifestyle. The sun raises everything on the land to its feet and makes it flourish. Those who drive, exercise and stretch themselves when the morning sun rises ascend the first step to success. These individuals have succeeded and ruled the world so far and will continue to do so in the future. If you consider yourself diligent, you must ask yourself if you have ever risen in the morning and greeted the sun when things went wrong at work and when you were physically unfit. The sun is the source of life. We can become healthier and summon good fortune just by looking at the rising sun.

What does it mean to have a boyfriend who lies on the bedroom floor while the sun is out, when he should be sitting up in case his father walks in? It's evident what kind of life awaits someone who lives with a man who doesn't seek new knowledge and isn't punctual for his appointments. Daughters should bear in mind the three questions I asked earlier when they are looking for men, and parents with sons have done their job if they have taught their sons these three things.

'You should start losing some weight and find a new boyfriend!' I said.

I don't know if my niece had caught my drift or was persuaded by a ticket to Europe, but a few months later she worked zealously to shed some weight, became a charming lady again as before, and dumped her lazy boyfriend. When my second son heard I was bringing his cousin to Europe – where he had never been – he said half with envy and half with sarcasm, 'Good for my cousin. She has a wealthy uncle…'

15

The Man Who Entrusts His Wife to His Friend

My wife has close friends with whom she often hangs out. Her friends freely call me 'older brother'. I have gladly played my role as a real older brother to them. Their husbands are all Americans, including one who is an eminent doctor and top executive at the University of Texas MD Anderson Cancer Center, and one who is a film director. Thanks to our wives, we husbands have hung out together and become close friends too.

One evening, when six of us were hanging out and having dinner together, the women dragged the men – who couldn't sing – to the karaoke bar. In the karaoke room, my exuberant wife swapped partners and started to dance with a friend's husband. Hopeless at dancing, I sat next to the woman whose husband had been taken by my wife, and watched them dance.

'Mickey! They look great, don't they?'

'Yes, they look great. The two of them look so lovely…'

It dawned on me for the first time at that instant on that day. That if this was all I had, I had succeeded. I didn't know what it felt like to be successful, even though I was growing my business and multiplying my assets and income. I didn't know what the benchmark of success was, because there were always a good many bigger businesses or more established entrepreneurs around me. Wealth, conventionally a clear benchmark of success, might have given me a sense of security, but it didn't move my heart.

Someone can envy me, but I can't earn their respect. However, I realised that I can feel secure and touched, be envied and respected, in candid friendships like these. These aren't relationships where we are conscious of who will be footing the bill; instead I worry whether I will get to pay this time round.

Sometimes one husband brings three women on a date. Another asks to borrow our wives on his way to work, and brings all of them on a plane with him. We also play pranks on one another by abruptly invading one couple's home at daybreak on a Sunday and then waking the sleeping people to make breakfast. We meet at one home on the weekends, where my friends expound Michael Pollan and Richard Dawkins while I endeavour to explain Laozi's philosophy. When we grow bored, we just tell silly jokes. Meanwhile, in one corner, our wives pile up empty wine bottles and guffaw.

We are family friends. We are like a family – our friends, their spouses and children. I have never seen what is written on the business cards of these friends.

I know that renowned figures in the United States line up to be operated on by Gary, and that the names of the celebrities William meets when filming a new movie are widely known. They are respected because of their social standing, but in our midst, they become delivery persons bringing newly bought bread, or coffee-brewing baristas.

I feel a real sense of success in life when I feel that I am always surrounded by people who can laugh with me. When I know that they will protect me and I will defend them should anything happen, I feel a real sense of success. It gives me an exhilarating sense of success when I am respected by people who are held in high esteem in this world.

One day, my lawyer told me I needed to appoint a custodian to manage my assets according to my will in case I met with any mishap. This also encompassed responsibility for my wife and children after my death. Gary came first to my mind. One day, when I was thinking of asking Gary to be the legal custodian of my estate and was looking for an opportunity to broach the question, Gary drew closer and said he needed to speak to me. He too wanted me to take care of his wife and children should he meet with an accident, and he asked if he could appoint me legal custodian of his estate. We each became the person to whom we will entrust our wives and children if we pass on first. A wager began that neither of us wanted to win.

Back to the karaoke room. Gary, a towering man, stood face to face with my wife and stuck out his buttocks as far as he could to dance with her. I linked arms with Gary's wife and sat guffawing. Have I succeeded? I think I have. What about you?

16

The Usefulness of Studying History and Geography

I lost my way in a forest of buildings in Shinjuku, Japan, but fortunately there was a map at the corner of a four-way intersection. I was delighted to see the map, because the hotel was in the vicinity but I didn't know the directions. However, my present location wasn't indicated on the map. When I simply walked according to guesswork, I saw another map. This time my present location was indicated on the map, but I didn't know which way was north. Because the map was written in Japanese.

Shinjuku's maps weren't useful to foreigners who couldn't read Japanese. Cursing my dead phone battery, I eventually located the hotel after much asking around. We must know our current location and the four cardinal points – north, south, east and west – if we wish to look at a map and find our way. We can't find our way without these two coordinates. We need a time and place when setting up an appointment. Without these two coordinates, we will be waiting or wandering forever.

As a CEO, the things that I must learn increase over time. The list is endless: accountancy, finance, economics, arts and humanities, law, exchange rates, labour management, real estate, psychology and so on. But I need two coordinates to apply what I have learned in business or life. The two coordinates are none other than history and geography. When we study these other subjects without learning history and geography, everything we have learned resembles a building constructed without foundations. We reduce ourselves to fundamentalists when we read the Bible without studying history and geography, and we are unable to perceive the editor's intention when we read a news article without historical and geographical knowledge. When we study seemingly completely unrelated subjects such as accountancy, exchange rates, maths, statistics and so on without historical and geographical knowledge, we learn nothing but numbers. It isn't easy to grasp these subjects because we are oblivious of the fact that contentious issues differ according to time and place.

When an earthquake strikes the United States, I receive calls from South Korea enquiring if I am all right. This is because the callers don't know that the distance between Houston and San Francisco is greater than that between Busan, South Korea, and Hong Kong. Guinea and Liberia, where the Ebola virus occurred, are in West Africa. Uninformed about which part of the continent it is, or how vast the African continent is, some people are under the illusion that all Africans are at risk of infection. They therefore don't welcome nationals from the Republic of South Africa, Ethiopia or Morocco, because they are from Africa. The truth is South Africa's Cape Town is as far from Guinea as is the United States' Miami. Russia's Vladivostok is closer to Fukushima, where the radiation disaster occurred, than is Kumamoto in southern Japan. Just having this geographical knowledge is tremendously useful for us to make rational and sensible judgements.

If geography is the study of space, history is the study of time. We feel as if the 1592 Japanese invasion of Korea, or the 1623 coup that put Injo of Joseon on the Korean throne, happened very long ago; but in fact, Christopher Columbus travelled across the Americas a century before these events took place, and Jumong founded the Kingdom of Goguryeo on the Korean peninsula around the time that Jesus was born. The Great Wall of China, which still exists today, was connected two centuries before the time of Jesus's ministry, which has been regarded as legend. The Aztec civilisation, which is often described as prehistoric, existed more than a century later than Oxford University, and disintegrated more than a century after King Sejong promulgated the Korean alphabet. Confucius, Laozi, Shakyamuni and Socrates were almost contemporaneous historically, and Jesus was born four centuries after the death of Socrates, who was the youngest of those four. Even if we don't specialise in historical studies, our thinking and judgements change surprisingly when we come to appreciate the chronology of world history.

When I was young, I received a book called *The Atlas* that resembled a literary supplement. It was a book that illustrated all sorts of maps and historical events with various charts. This book isn't used as a textbook in schools. But it's one of the must-read books for entrepreneurs. We can never make level-headed judgements without understanding history and geography. Those who follow ordinary insights can never pull ahead in business. When there are changes and distortions, historical and geographical knowledge proves its usefulness, and a business is formed in the process of identifying and rectifying these changes and distortions.

17

Rescheduling an Appointment Is No Different from Being Late

I once wrote a short article titled 'Twenty-Six Lessons for My Sons', which became quite popular. The first line of the article was 'Do not run a business with people who are late for appointments'. It was a lesson I had learned after being disappointed a couple of times with business partners who were always late for appointments. From then on, as I highlighted in my article, I have also been conscientious about showing up punctually for appointments, and I have always equally respected an appointment for a business deal worth several hundred million dollars and an appointment at a hairdresser's.

This guiding principle for appraising my business partners, employees and friends has always been useful and valuable, even today. I no longer expect anything from people who are slightly late for no reason. Conversely, I appraise positively those who always show up on time, and they live up to my expectations too. The intriguing thing is that many people think they are punctual, although punctual people are rare. These people are mistaken on two counts. For instance, they presume they are punctual even when they turn up at 3.05 p.m. or 3.10 p.m. for a 3 p.m. appointment. And they think being a tad late isn't really being late. If we want to be precise, showing up at 3.01 p.m. is still showing up late.

These people maintain a so-what attitude, even if they are one day late paying their bills. They can't understand that to someone else, that one day might strangle them to death as surely as a rope around their neck. There are also people who don't arrive late but reschedule appointments.

'There is a traffic jam on my way there. Can we delay our appointment by about thirty minutes?'

'Something has cropped up today. Can't we meet in the afternoon?'

They are very polite, but the other party is unable to do anything in that thirty minutes, schedule other appointments or commit to other work. But it's also senseless to ask someone who has said beforehand that they will be thirty minutes late to come again next time. The person who is thirty minutes late considers themselves to be a punctual person because they have kindly notified us beforehand. They are also proud of being considerate of the other party by notifying them in advance. This is an absurd attitude.

I give almost the same credibility scores to people who don't show up, who are late, and who reschedule appointments at the last minute. If you wish to succeed in business, I advise you again and again: do not be late. Do not be even a minute late. Do not reschedule appointments. Never reschedule appointments, particularly on the day itself. And maintain this attitude throughout your life. Apply this to all your appointments with bosses, business partners, hairdressers, restaurants, friends, family, children, lectures, theatrical performances, social gatherings and so on.

If you have promised your wife 'I will be home in ten minutes', then be home in ten minutes, even if you must sprint. If the husband is a person who arrives home exactly in ten minutes, dinner can be served on time, and the wife won't need to go to the trouble of reheating the stew several times over. The person who conscientiously shows up punctually for appointments takes a shortcut to success.

[5] Seung-Ho Kim, *Jagigyeongyeong noteul* [Note on Self-Management] (Seoul: Hwanggeumsaja, 2009).

18

Your Destiny Changes When You Straighten Your Back

Employees at luxury stores have their own guidelines for ascertaining whether the customers who visit their stores are buyers or purely sightseers. Many people visit luxury stores out of curiosity and are eager to spot hidden price tags. There is a surprisingly simple way of identifying those among the curious that are genuine buyers with whom employees should exchange more eye contact and to whom they should pay more attention.

When humans are accustomed to raising their social status and receiving favourable treatment, they straighten their backs and move unhurriedly. Straightening one's back is a natural behaviour that makes one look somewhat bigger. Moving unhurriedly is an unconscious behaviour that tacitly determines a person's superiority by making others wait for them. In other words, these are refined and graceful comportments.

We must straighten our backs and move unhurriedly to look refined and graceful. I confirmed my assumption about luxury stores in an emporium to which I had accompanied my wife. Although I was well dressed, none of the employees looked at me when I shifted from place to place as though flitting between the stores. They assumed I would leave after looking around. However, when I straightened my shoulders and sauntered into the stores, although I was dressed in a T-shirt and a pair of jeans, they appeared with a bottle of Fiji Water for me. They told me to approach them if I needed help, and stood at a comfortable distance a little behind me, ready to assist me. I realised this human behaviour clearly had nothing to do with attire, age or race, but was to do with being respected by others. I could no longer continue this mischief of mine, because a sales employee had promptly memorised my name when I couldn't resist a pair of brown shoes that matched my jeans.

An older male cousin of mine complained, 'Why do dogs run away when they see me?' He wondered if dogs knew he detested them as soon as they met him. Dogs have a way of discerning people who call them sons of bitches. Surprisingly, they can discern whether someone adores dogs or treats them carelessly, just by observing subtle changes of gesture. They can tell whether someone is hostile or friendly just by the position of the back of their hand, little changes in shoulder movements, movements of the shins when the person is walking and so on. Surprisingly, they can sense whether an approaching hand wants to grab or stroke them. Our resolve to do something is expressed through our bodies. Therefore, this ability would be essential to dogs, as their survival depends on it. But dogs aren't the only ones who possess this ability.

Humans have a similar ability too. Thus, when I straighten my back and pull my shoulders wide before moving unhurriedly on, others feel as if they 'should respect this person'. They think they ought to be cautious because I am not someone who behaves carelessly. When anyone adopts this practice, although they may not be a remarkable person now, the people around them will start to perceive them as though they are, and they will eventually become remarkable. The reason is our appearance supports our attitudes, our attitudes alter our behaviours, and our behaviours transform our destinies. Conversely, when I hunch or slouch, everyone belittles me and no one respects me, and if I grow accustomed to this life, it goes without saying that I will accept it.

When we hurry and flurry, we make frequent mistakes and are reproached. When we are in a restaurant, we should avoid dropping crumbs on the table. Do not wolf down your food. Do not eat noisily. Do not smack your lips or slurp your food. And whatever your posture, always remember that you transform your destiny just by straightening your back and pulling your shoulders wide. Success doesn't come in one fell swoop with the vast wisdom of life. Small but good habits cumulate and lead a person to success. If you have read this, I hope you will straighten your hunched back once again.

19

Desk Drawers, Car Boot and Wallet

There are three items we must always organise to succeed as CEOs.

When we consider the wallets that men stuff into their back pockets, they are thicker than we think. There are occasions when they are thick because cash has been stashed inside them, but when we open them up, the majority of it turns out to be business cards that the owners have received from somewhere. Women carry long purses that display all sorts of cards and receipts on both sides, as if they were carrying a pregnant yellow corvina in their handbags. Nowadays, overweight executives aren't welcome, because they somehow project the image of idleness. The same applies to wallets. Overweight wallets don't look like they contain abundant information and wealth, but project the image of an idle and disorganised person.

Someone who has a thick wad of cash comes across as having a dubious rather than a successful business. It suffices for a wallet to have one or two cards, one or two bills of the largest value, and business cards. Everything else should be organised and left at home or in the office. I bet everyone has one of these from a year ago: business cards of individuals whose names you have forgotten, pieces of receipts whose print has faded, toothpicks, and condoms for unforeseen romantic encounters. Things that you carry around, thinking you might use them someday, will hurt your back. For those whose back often hurts on one side for no reason: the pain will dissipate once the wallet in your back pocket has been lightened. This is because your strained buttocks will be able to stand upright again.

Desk drawers should also be organised regularly. You should make it easy to always find whatever you need in the drawers. And it's unlikely that someone who doesn't organise their desk drawers will organise their computer files.

You might have had the experience of combing through every hard drive to find one file, and when that didn't work, looking through black kite bird, woodpecker, red-crowned crane and ibis.[6] Let's separate and organise tax documents that must be kept safe, legal documents, receipts that can be discarded several years later, stationery and so on. Let's not feel wasteful about pens or highlighters that have completely run out of ink, and discard them. You should collect batteries in one place, based on their sizes, to avoid buying them again. Organised drawers are a yardstick of how you manage your assets.

The last thing to get in order is the car boot. To sum up, there are a few simple things that should always be kept in the car boot. These are simply supplies in case of an emergency, and a spare pair of trainers for changing out of your shoes. Everything else should be unloaded from the car. People will be astonished when they come to realise how many things they have in the car boot and how long they have been there. The car boot should always be emptied. An entirely empty car boot shows how conscientious a person you are.

Looks clearly don't tell us everything about a person. These three items – drawers, car boot and wallet – teach us about emptying. Only by emptying can we be filled.

---

6   Translator's note: These bird names are the names of desktop folders created with software called ALZip, which has a feature to name a new folder after a type of bird. It might be a jesting play on words, as 'new' also means 'bird' in Korean.

The person who is unable to empty what is unneeded and organise their life can't take in what is needed, even if they obtain it. If you can verify these three items in your search for a partner, employee or son-in-law, you will be a tad more assured of your future.

20

How to Make Others Quietly Detest You

I can make everyone detest me if I behave in certain ways. There are techniques to increase the number of people who aren't appreciative even if I buy them food and alcohol, who don't show me respect even if I hire them, and who quietly disobey me in everything, as well as to prevent them from contacting me before I contact them. If you apply these techniques well, no one will invite you to officiate at their wedding even if you have aged with dignity, and your subordinates will speak ill of you behind your back. They won't contact you for the rest of their lives once they leave the company. Though these techniques aren't as simple as we think, a significant number of people have instinctively learned and acquired them. It's like speaking Korean fluently even without learning its grammar.

Now I will carefully describe the techniques for the purpose of reviewing them. Always interrupt when someone is talking. Barge in when many people are talking and instantly change the subject. Once you draw others onto your subject, swiftly change the subject again. Those who are somewhat more skilful pretend to listen and, responding half-heartedly, abruptly change the subject again. When something or a remark worth boasting about surfaces in conversation, the ingenious way is to quickly focus on that subject and quietly blow your own trumpet, then back off. If you know a technical term or recall some statistics, blurt them out all at once. If someone says they are unwell, pretend you are in greater pain, and offer comfort later. When subordinates err, remind them of what they have done now and what they did three years ago. If you skilfully use these techniques on your wife or husband, you might end in divorce. At the very least, you might get hit on the back.

Praise yourself extensively when an opportunity presents itself. If you have given someone a gift, brag to those around you about having given the gift. And always remind the recipient of the gift. In particular, always personally boast to your wife's family when you have presented your wife with a gift. Chat for two hours on subjects that others are uninterested in, or talk non-stop about your personal concerns. You can also fish out photos of your daughter or grandson and show them to someone you are meeting for the first time, and talk about the schools they have recently enrolled in or the certificates they have received so far.

Using phrases like 'That's nothing' or 'Listen to me' once every three minutes works like a charm. There are 'discord' or 'exaggeration' techniques you can use to induce a reaction, the earliest in a few days, or longer in a few years. Others will use these techniques anyway, but even if they don't, you mustn't show up and admit that you have sown discord between people and feel sorry about it. The good thing about sowing discord between people is that those who are affected don't even realise it, because they rarely insist on conferring with one another.

Always offer a conclusion when women are talking, and check if your explicit solution has been properly implemented. Always lament and whine to a senior or your friend. No one will bother you if you do this several times. Repeat the same story until you feel that it has been conveyed. This is effective only if you repeat the same story at least three or four times. It will be impeccable if you repeat it once more the next time you meet them.

It requires considerable effort and study to make others detest us. You must start applying these techniques right now if you don't want people to visit and bother you when you grow old, and if you don't want to needlessly build a business that will become an inheritance problem and cause chaos among your children. You can only succeed if you entirely ignore the Korean saying that we should speak less and keep our wallets open as we age. But I am deeply concerned as to whether you will unconsciously pay full attention to this lengthy essay of mine.

21

Do Not Apply for Credit Cards

There are two groups of people living in this era of financial capitalism. One group pays interest to banks, and the other receives interest from banks. But interest receivers and interest payers aren't differentiated by income. Their difference lies in whether they use future earnings or past earnings. It depends on the type of earnings they use. People who pay interest to banks use future earnings, and those who receive interest use past earnings.

I teach my children, nieces and nephews not to apply for credit cards. As soon as children become adults, they naturally yearn to own credit cards on which their names are beautifully imprinted. It feels as if credit cards are certificates that will usher them into the adult world. But the reality is that ninety percent of people begin to pay interest and form queues at banks for the rest of their lives the moment they apply for credit cards. I don't know what the younger ones have heard and from where, but they ask me how they can improve their credit scores. The truth is that credit scores are useless except when one is applying for a loan. A credit score doesn't measure a person's actual credibility; it's a criterion that assesses how well a person can repay money borrowed from financial institutions. The person with the highest credibility is someone who has no debts because their assets far outweigh their liabilities. In the case of credit scores, however, financial institutions slightly distort this and give the highest scores to those who repay well after taking a loan.

I have always warned young people that it's tremendously risky to apply for credit cards and take out loans to purchase cars just to improve their credit scores, even though they don't have any specific liabilities now. This is because the crossroads between receiving interest and paying interest for the rest of our lives starts here. I don't own a personal credit card. I have only a personal debit card and a corporate card in the thin, single-layered wallet in my pocket. I have instructed my company to pay the full balance on the corporate card every month, so we don't pay the bank any interest at all. I have the worst credit score. The reason is I don't have a record with the banks in the first place.

When banks give the worst credit ratings to people who have the highest credibility in the real world, it shows that we aren't customers if we haven't borrowed money from them. Of course, this is the worst credit rating to them. You might then ask how we could purchase houses and cars in this modern society if we ignored credibility, as I have suggested. I have a simple solution.

Wait until there is cash. Set aside cash assiduously. If you don't have enough cash to purchase a new car, get a second-hand one. If you don't have enough cash to purchase a house, live in a small rented house. Do not care about the types of houses that your friends or other entrepreneurs live in and the lives they lead. They are, after all, merely captives of financial institutions who are using their future earnings.

Although I had given the employees who had achieved our company goals a BMW each, I had no personal cash and was driving a worn-out truck for a couple of years. I wasn't bothered, even when I heard someone say, 'That guy is still living in destitution although his business is thriving.' I didn't consider recklessly taking a loan to finance the purchase of an office building, even when around twenty employees were sharing desks and rubbing cheek by jowl in a small 783-square-foot office with two rooms.

Only after we had paid in cash did we move into a 35,600-square-foot office on a 107,000-square-foot piece of land, where everyone got their own spacious desk. I also often purchased houses without taking loans, after I had set aside enough cash and searched for houses that I could purchase with the amount of cash I could spend. I didn't apply for the commonplace department store and petrol station cards. In any case, I didn't want to go anywhere near an interest-paying lifestyle. This thought process didn't come about when I was making money and my business was thriving.

I am someone who has failed countless times. Through the processes of failures, I correct and learn from my mistakes. I decided on this behavioural credo when I was at my lowest and had a great number of debts, and I never looked back after doing my utmost to pay off all the debts.

One of the best decisions I have made since entering the business world is to live without paying interest. If I hadn't eagerly adopted this lifestyle back then, I would have come up with numerous excuses to take out loans to run a business again, and bitten off more than I could chew by purchasing an office building or a house that matched the size of my business. I have no debt, not even a dollar. I have already paid for everything I have. Even if I go bankrupt now, no one will come after me or call me. That said, I have a dreadful credit score. Banks fret because they are unable to issue me a loan; on the other hand, I bargain for and receive higher interest rates from banks, irrespective of their publicly published rates.

As an entrepreneur, I don't wish to attach this reasoning to business loans that utilise business leverage. I know full well that banks clearly have favourable functions as banks, and businesses can expand and grow thanks to these functions. It's only fair that profits are shared with banks through interest. But I urge you never to think of spending interest on personal matters or personal possessions, but to preserve its value throughout your life.

In the modern economy, no matter how conscientious we have been, everything can disappear instantly in a financial structure that can change

'I didn't consider recklessly taking a loan to finance the purchase of an office building, even when around twenty employees were sharing desks and rubbing cheek by jowl in a small 783-square-foot office with two rooms. Only after we had paid in cash did we move into a 35,600-square-foot office on a 107,000-square-foot piece of land, where everyone got their own spacious desk.'

96 • *Grab and Go*

in a flash. There is no other way to protect ourselves and our assets and free ourselves from these risks throughout our lives but to completely eradicate all personal debts. The first step is not applying for credit cards.

The person who is suitable to apply for credit cards is simply someone who has the ability or takes action to pay the full balance every month. People who have paid instalments over three or six months, at least once in their lives, should never own credit cards. All the points developed by credit card companies aren't meant to benefit you; they are mere bait to reel you in, like fish hooked on rods. Once you are hooked, they will be reeling you in all your life, till the day you die.

Credit cards hold your future earnings as collateral. The future can never safeguard the present. But the present can safeguard the future. If you plan to heed my advice only when your income is somewhat higher, as you don't have an alternative measure now, I am certain you won't have the determination to do so even if your income does indeed increase. Because this isn't a matter of income level. Cut up your credit card with a pair of scissors right now, and apply for a debit card. Those who are unable to do so should clench their teeth and fight to free themselves from the fishing hooks in their mouths. Entrepreneurs in particular will eventually imperil their families if they aren't aware of such matters. Now I hope you will close this book for a moment and fetch a pair of scissors.

22

Resistance to Formalised Ideas

I don't like to work out using exercise machines. Exercises that build muscles by using machines that follow fixed trajectories lose the original purpose of exercise. Exercise isn't meant to build impressive muscles. The purpose of exercise is to keep our body healthy, in optimal condition. Muscles are a by-product, not the purpose of exercise.

When I do push-ups, the muscles I use in my everyday life get to work. Every time, my body cooperates organically with each individual muscle, depending on the reach of my open arms and the angle of my feet, and every time my body is fine-tuned. My entire body is tense, especially my arm muscles. However, when I do chest exercises using machines, it doesn't train the rest of my muscles. I can thoroughly use and tense all my muscles just by doing three exercises: push-ups, sit-ups and squats. These exercises can be done anywhere, and a large space isn't needed. It's possible to do them just by spreading a towel beside a hotel bed. But young people nowadays think they should visit the gym if they wish to exercise and, if they do, they must use the exercise machines or lift weights. For this reason, they pay gym membership fees, and when they start coming up with excuses not to go, they stop exercising altogether. The idea that to exercise is to visit the gym and to visit the gym is to exercise has already become formalised.

One formalised idea is 'It's difficult to run a business in a recession'. In recent years, I haven't seen anyone whose business is thriving in South Korea. The truth is we are fearful of the persistent recession. And the percentage is much higher than expected: nine out of ten South Korean business owners say that their businesses haven't performed as well as in previous years, and that there are no signs that things will improve in the future. But the fascinating thing is, if we look around us, it's always hard to book tickets at the cinema, and the major commercial districts are always teeming with people. The roads are congested on Saturday mornings because of the people going out to play, and airports declare that the number of people travelling overseas is the highest ever.

A recession is usually not a period of dreadful anxiety when one in three people is unemployed, as happened during the Great Depression. The latter happens once a century. Although most are called long-term recessions, they are ten-year periods of either low growth or slight economic decline. But why do individual entrepreneurs or small and medium-sized businesses work so hard, to the point of frustration? The reason is they perceive recessions as an inevitable, limitless force, and they don't resist them. The Japanese-owned convenience store chain 7-Eleven grows in a recession. The company believes that economic prosperity is good and a recession better. Even in a recession, customers dress themselves, eat and play.

In a recession, people spend generously on things that are important to them, and if possible spend the rest of their money to sustain a pattern of frugal 'flexible consumption'. They will buy an exorbitant slice of cake that costs more than a meal to cheer themselves up. The idea that a recession is unfavourable to doing business stems from a lack of understanding of the essential character of business. A recession is actually springtime for exceptional entrepreneurs to do business. This is because numerous competitors will already have pulled back and are hardly thinking of investing. Many companies set restrictions on their services and lower their product quality on the pretext of a recession. They simply let go and leave the customers alone.

The saying that we should continue learning throughout our lives is also one of the most misunderstood. People are liberal about learning. This is because we firmly believe that learning is one of the beautiful virtues. But the fact is we should quit learning if we don't intend to pursue knowledge as a scholar does. As a child we attend taekwondo, mental arithmetic and English classes; as a young adult we go for yoga, Test of English for International Communication (TOEIC) or Photoshop classes, study for civil service exams and so on; then when we grow old we sign up for photography, humanities, social dancing, stock investment, auction methods and singing classes, as well as all kinds of high-level university courses and so on. The list is endless.

The 'isn't it good to learn everything?' defence is lost on parents, spouses or children who have observed such acts of learning from the sidelines all their lives. They have absolutely no respect for mothers or fathers who love learning so much that they are often out and about. They therefore lead reclusive lives, and mistrust abounds. Learning should produce results. The person who attends consecutive seminars throughout their life and collects countless certificates without producing results – in other words, making learning the purpose of their life – is unable to achieve anything independently or to lead others. There is value in learning only when it's done so we can think independently and produce results. We should stop taking all sorts of lessons from others, being persuaded one moment to buy and collect certain equipment, then persuaded the next moment to bring home an armful of textbooks. Learning resembles the bucket of water that is poured into the Korean traditional pump to draw water from the ground. It should take only three or four bowls of water to fill a bucket. Learning isn't always good for everyone. I hope we will stop indulging our gullible selves on the pretext of learning.

Oddly, in life we don't always do as well as others, although we should if we think and act the same way they do. If you aspire to live as others do, you must think and act differently from them. If you wish to be far more outstanding than others, the first step is to acquire the habit of questioning everything that has already been formalised in this world.

23

The Courage to Change Your Mind

I recently observed an interesting scene after stopping by a downtown shopping mall. An elderly black man walking ahead of me stopped abruptly when he saw two young people walking towards us from the opposite side. He was shaking his head and scowling at them, all the while standing motionless until they passed from sight. The elderly man's forehead said 'Young people nowadays…', and the corners of his eyes said 'What has the world come to?' The elderly man's eyes were filled with contempt. Tolerance and understanding of homosexuality have grown significantly compared with the past, but it seemed difficult for him to accept two twenty-year-old men openly holding hands and walking together affectionately.

The elderly black man had clearly experienced the anguish of being part of a minority and a disadvantaged group since he was young. But his own perceptions of other minorities remained unchanged. Even his experience as a member of an ethnic minority couldn't alter his perception of a sexual minority. He had perceived the behaviour of the young men as independent of ethnicity and sexual orientation. But we should understand this matter from the angle of tolerance for minorities. This is because any of us could fall into a minority category, anytime, anywhere. I am simply a South Korean when I am in South Korea, but I fall into the Asian migrant minority category as soon as I step into an American airport.

Male nurses are a minority in hospitals where female nurses abound. Contract employees are a minority in the workplace. People who have recently moved in are a minority in the neighbourhood. Those who have new ideas are also a minority. Persons with disabilities are a minority on the roads. New members are a minority in a club. People of mixed race are also a minority in countries such as South Korea. Transfer students are a minority in schools, and travellers are a minority where they travel. We can't always be part of the majority. We therefore live by relying on the tolerance of others. A society without tolerance for minorities and disadvantaged groups resembles a knife pointed at oneself.

I am not a homosexual. But I am cautious of heterosexuals who thoughtlessly insult or arbitrarily judge homosexuals. This is because if they haven't yet learned tolerance in this matter, they will also view other matters with a closed and parochial mindset. In particular, soldiers, police officers and civil servants who work for the public interest of countless people, as well as company presidents and managers who deal with many subordinates, should embrace the spirit of tolerance, as Zhuangzi did.[7]

Tolerance extended to others, after all, is tolerance extended to oneself. If this tolerance spreads across society, my child won't be bullied when he transfers to a new school, and our daughters won't be ridiculed when they look for a new job. Kindness extended to travellers is desperately helpful when I travel, and I am free from being condemned as a lunatic if I am drawn to new ideas or religions. People who thoughtlessly insult homosexuals in private might someday desperately need the private tolerance of others.

There is no need to feel ashamed about changing your mind. The truly shameful thing is not having the courage to change your mind.

---

7 Zhuangzi is a pivotal figure in philosophical Daoism, who sees tolerance and flexibility as salient values in life.

24

A Conversation with Panda Express CEO Andrew Cherng

As a CEO and leader of an organisation, I had never once expressed my fears about any difficulty. I worried that the entire organisation would feel insecure, and that insecurity would lead to adverse consequences, if I showed that I was afraid of something. But I visited Andrew's room with a notebook and asked him to coach me as my senior in life and business. Andrew gladly brewed tea and sat with me.

'I am a little afraid now.'

'What are you afraid of?'

As CEO of the Panda Restaurant Group, and an entrepreneur with twenty thousand employees and a chain of one thousand five hundred restaurants, Andrew – who sports a crew cut and speaks in a firm, strong voice – has been considered one of the most successful Chinese entrepreneurs in the United States.

'Over the past six years, our company has grown from one to three hundred stores. But we plan to open between five hundred and a thousand stores in the next year. I am concerned whether rapid expansion will be good for the company, and whether our employees and I will be able to competently run a company on this scale. Not only do I not have any experience operating a company on a nationwide scale, but our employees have no professional management experience either, as all of them have learned from scratch together.'

I did want to boast about the terrifying growth of my new business to this sixty-five-year-old man, who had nowhere further to climb on the ladder and had arrived at the peak of his business career. But I was also really afraid.

I was eager to know what he would say about my bold boasting. I believed that natural entrepreneurs were rare on this earth, and that anyone could operate a large-scale business even if they hadn't received a professional education, but I was still curious about what he thought.

However, he questioned me instead. In a tatami room at a spring in Hakone, Japan, where the sun was already setting, I started to have trouble answering his questions.

'Did your employees become better people after they met you?'

When I hesitated to respond, he continued.

'What is the percentage of cost price in the markup of product prices in your business?'

After hearing my reply, he said, 'Someone is making a huge profit.' He was cool-headed as usual. I supposed the person who was making a huge profit might not be me.

'Three parties should be satisfied in this business. You know that, don't you?'

I knew. I always used to explain it to our employees, using the legs of a stool as an example: 'All three parties – companies that give us work, store owners who work with us, and our company – must be satisfied for the stool to stand on its own. If any of its legs is shorter than the others, the stool will fall. Please work hard to satisfy all three of them.' I answered his question confidently, because I knew better than anyone else that our competitors hadn't been able to beat us across the whole of America and had foundered, because they didn't have a structure that satisfied all three parties.

'You are aware. If I substituted your business with mine, the three parties would be landlords, employees and me.'

As soon as he had paid me a small compliment, he asked again.

'But there is one more party. There is one more party that must be satisfied, just as there are often four instead of three legs to a stool. Do you know who that is?'

When I hesitated to answer again, he pulled a stool close to him, sat down and answered his own question.

'Consumers, that is, customers. Your cost price is very low. It won't satisfy customers to have a low cost price and a high profit. You will have the whole market to yourself now, as your competitors are able to satisfy only one or two legs, but your customers will leave if this continues in the future. In the end, someone will take over your place someday.'

Andrew was right. I had excluded my customers by emphasising the profits to the three parties.

His judgements and intellect were lucid and sharp. I came to believe that the Panda Restaurant Group wasn't a company that had risen by chance and good fortune. I had clearly not considered the interests of customers until this meeting. The truth was I hadn't been able to do that, because maximising profits for the three parties had been the only way to defeat my competitors. But my business would cease to exist someday if I ignored the consumers. Because a stool with four legs is more secure than one with three. The quiet lesson in that tatami room in Japan made me realise the need to complete the last leg of my business. I couldn't dismiss his business prowess.

25

Jack Georges Bags

I bought a black leather briefcase which was neither big nor small. I usually bought bags to store things, but I simply bought this bag without having thought about what it should store. It's an exceedingly ordinary product, with a metal chain and lock on the front; when I open it, the interior is partitioned into several compartments. The brand name Jack Georges is imprinted on a metal button in a corner of the bag.

I had no idea who Jack Georges was before this. Based on what I gathered from an elderly saleswoman who sold bags and had started working again after her husband had passed on, a designer who used to work for a luxury bag company had left the company to found Jack Georges.

It's evident that there are no lavish accessories or outstanding designs on Jack Georges bags. But at a glance I could sense their exceptional needlework and material quality. My wife was curious why someone who hadn't carried a bag in his life would spend the small fortune of $300 on this bag. I wanted to explain, but I might have sounded long-winded, so I said, 'Just because it's pretty.' But I knew why as soon as I saw the bag.

Bags show signs of wear as soon as we purchase them. I knew there would be scratches, stains and discolouration in various places. But I also knew that this bag wouldn't get rumpled or squashed, thanks to its strong leather and painstaking needlework. I bought it in a heartbeat, because I sensed it would be the kind of bag that looks more refined the more it is used and the more it wears out.

As I had expected, I grew more attached to the bag the more I carried it. The number of scratch marks caused by my fingernails has grown, and it looks somewhat dishevelled, but it appears more refined than when I first bought it. I brought this bag along when I travelled to dozens of states in the United States, and it travelled with me not just to Alaska but also to numerous foreign countries. There is a pocket at the back of the bag where it can hold my small laptop securely and I can easily get it whenever I need to, and it has a broad strap that I can sling over my shoulder comfortably for long hours.

I believe there are people who resemble this bag. Youth and beauty are temporary, but there are people who become better beings as they grow older. There are people who remain beautiful and exceedingly dignified despite their wrinkles.

Friends who are more awesome as they grow older and more valuable as time passes aren't burdens on my shoulders, no matter how close we are. Rather, I am proud that they are standing on my shoulders.

26

Why South Korean Franchises Should Enter the US Market

South Korean franchises have been expanding rapidly over the last decade. They have evolved surprisingly in quality and quantity. If you have recently visited an exhibition of South Korean franchises, you will have seen that they are more dynamic and creative than franchises from other developed countries. But the first franchise companies in South Korea were suspected as scams. There was endless confusion as they recruited store owners while the royalties-based income structure was still unclear, and they maintained an unusual income structure based on interior fees or supply distribution.

Rather than keeping franchises perennially alive, these early franchises operated in a hit-and-run style. They neglected store owners, and they no longer offered any support or help to develop the businesses once they had collected the franchise fees and opened a multitude of stores. It was also common for them to operate in the same style with a second brand. Recently, however, the Korea Franchise Association has been revamped to focus on the owners of major mid-sized companies, and has grown to become a substantial organisation that resembles a fraternal society. It has commissioned university courses for CEOs, strengthened its internal standards, and strived to establish itself as a substantial industry player.

In addition, as perceptive young entrepreneurs join the franchise industry in droves, relationships with store owners, operating standards and so on have been reformed remarkably. Employee welfare and salary structures have also improved significantly, and countless talented people have been recruited. The store designs and operating methods of some of the top companies are surprisingly refined and structured, keeping pace with the franchise industry in developed countries. Hygiene and employee training have also been improved substantially. As the introduction of these new stores is coinciding with the 'Korean wave', they have received numerous offers from companies in South-East Asia and the greater China region. It's just like three decades ago, when the craze for Japanese and American instant noodles switched to Korean noodles. The Chinese market looks like an easy mark when business leaders visit China to conduct market research. They are in a hurry to enter the Chinese market because they don't see any competitors, and the potential customers seem endless.

That said, I remain critical of South Korean franchises entering the Chinese market. My reasons are as follows: first, the business infrastructure is weak. It's like exporting to a country without harbours or roads. Even if companies manufacture goods in China, it seems there are no proper roads to transport them, and there are inadequate facilities to moor ships to load and unload goods. It's a fact that legislation evolves swiftly with the political climate, and the practical challenges that arise irrespective of legislation are formidable. In the end, it's hard to extract the profits even if your business thrives, the protection of property rights is equivocal, and there is no state organisation from which you can receive practical help.

Second, it's hard to decide on a marketing focus, as the population is colossal and lifestyle differences are drastic. The wealthy are exceedingly wealthy, and there are innumerable poor people. If a company decides to market to wealthy people, there is only a small number of them, and the products will be overpriced if the company wants to reach out to the general public. It's impossible to sell high-end products to the general public, because they aren't highly recognisable brands. Companies are piggybacking on the Korean wave, but they have no idea how long this transient wave will last after they open their stores. Until the early 1980s, if you were to visit coffee shops in South Korea, you would find layers of gum stuck under the tables. This was South Koreans' 'hidden' level of public consciousness back then. Some American companies were prepared to enter the South Korean market only in the latter half of the 1980s, when the gum had disappeared.

IKEA has removed free pencils from its stores in South Korea. Fast-food restaurants have removed self-service beverage machines, and Costco has hidden its hotdog onions. These companies didn't know that the public consciousness of South Koreans had remained underdeveloped. The vestiges of the 1980s are still present in South Korea. China is a place where all levels of public consciousness, from the 1960s to the 2010s, still coexist. Employees who have a habit of spitting, and refined employees who have received a formal education in the West, work together in the stores. There are also diverse customers, from those who come in barefoot to people in Armani shoes.

Third, South Koreans exude a sense of superiority, even in business. One of the deplorable habits of South Korean entrepreneurs is their strong tendency to snub countries whose national power or earnings are lower than South Korea's. Therefore, they often implicitly snub South-East Asians and the Chinese, but tend not to treat Westerners carelessly. These attitudes are evident at travel destinations. South Koreans behave carelessly while touring the East, and speak condescendingly when they see something that displeases them; but they are silent and do as they are told when they are at travel destinations in the West. These conflicting attitudes towards Easterners and Westerners have an impact on business. Although it seems as if my company could dominate the Chinese market if we were to enter China, I am not confident of surpassing the high standards of Western markets. It seems we can even curse thoughtlessly at Eastern employees, but I am afraid when I think of dealing with Western employees.

The local enterprises in China have their reasons for preserving their businesses in their present state, irrespective of capital or business experience. If you look around their businesses, you find that they don't hang lighting over their merchandise, the employees have no uniforms, and personal hygiene is dreadful, as employees don't wash their hair before coming to work. I might rectify all these issues if I opened a store in China, but after visiting the country I realised there were diverse explanations for these issues: it takes a long time and kickbacks to set up new power lines; uniforms go missing after they have been given to employees; hygiene training is impracticable for lifestyle reasons, as employees live in environments where they are unable to shower every day.

We can never succeed in business if we snub Chinese customers and small company executives in China. Besides, business partners in China are entrepreneurs who are more competent and astute about partnerships than South Koreans. It's imprudent of South Korean franchises with no international branding power to do business with them. The Chinese can easily go independent by localising the relevant business models. We are now making the same mistakes in China as Japanese franchises have been making in South Korea over the past thirty years.

That said, many enterprising companies are already operating businesses in several major Asian cities, and some of them have set quite successful precedents. They must have worked tirelessly to overcome the three obstacles mentioned above. But there are still very few companies whose successes have led to actual exit strategies. Questions arise here. Why enter China and shoulder so much hardship and risk? Are the businesses manageable because China is geographically close? Is advertising in South Korea effective only if it's known that a company has stores in China too? Why is everyone charging forward even when it's evident that countless soldiers will die scaling the city walls, and there is no guarantee that they will leave with the spoils of war even if they climb over? If you deliberate on the answers to these questions, you can't help but think that South Korean franchises are yielding to romantic rather than entrepreneurial sentiments when they enter the Chinese market.

What I recommend as a solution is that South Korean franchises should enter the US market with the same passion. I know South Korean franchises can be very popular in the US market too. Noodle speciality shops, barbecue restaurants that serve beef slices or ribs, steamed seafood speciality shops, dumplings shops, *bingsoo* speciality shops, dessert cafés, coffee shops and products such as chicken are warmly welcomed by Americans. Of course, it isn't the case that these businesses haven't entered the US market. However, they have started primarily in Koreatowns where Koreans live, and they end up being globalised by the Korean diaspora. Some South Koreans have their relatives or friends in the United States set up stores without going through proper master franchise agreements, and some make the absurd mistake of losing their company names to store owners.

When South Koreans enter China, they aren't concerned about the Chinese diaspora market and they aim to localise their business, whereas their first consideration in the United States is to globalise their business. No doubt they might succeed if they were to register localised franchises and consider the locals as their area of business, as they have in China. Strictly speaking, South Korean franchises that have been globalised by the Korean diaspora can't be considered overseas expansion; nor are they able to employ American franchise business techniques.

Noodles are now an increasingly commonplace item in American markets. A considerable number of Americans now use chopsticks. Vietnam *pho*, Japanese ramen and so on have proliferated through mainstream markets year on year. Speciality shops where every kind of noodle from the East is assembled will likely be very popular. The grilling of beef slices and beef ribs

'I know South Korean franchises can be very popular in the US market too. Noodle speciality shops, barbecue restaurants that serve beef slices or ribs, steamed seafood speciality shops, dumplings shops, bingsoo speciality shops, dessert cafés, coffee shops and products such as chicken are warmly welcomed by Americans.'

right at the table is the best show business. This model is fully marketable not only in major cities, but in small and medium-sized cities too. The spectacle of making steamed dumplings will appeal to all classes and be hugely popular. *Bingsoo* is a fascinating item that offers a change to markets divided between ice cream and yoghurt, and dessert cafés will appeal to young consumers in major cities. All types of South Korean chicken, whether seasoned, grilled or fried, are second only to the best products in the United States. It's a real shame that these products are found only in South Korea.

In the case of coffee shops, their operation styles and store designs are as good as American ones – that is, if they cater to the tastes of American consumers. Compared with American franchises, South Korean franchises offer many more show-like elements that arouse interest. This is one of the greatest advantages during a business's initial growth. Furthermore, America is a colossal market where a business with a nationwide model can open as many as three thousand stores. This figure is nearly impossible in China, where the population is massive but income differences are dire and distribution unstable. Besides, America's biggest attraction is that businesses can be fully protected by law. This means we can be assured of and secure royalties, and be guaranteed of the most important income source in a franchise business. Store owners of course maintain fairness by paying these fees, subscribe to a rational business culture that honours contractual agreements, and don't distress themselves unnecessarily over business.

If you wish to operate a franchise business that has a rational business outlook, shares the profits between you and your store owners, and desires to grow, America is definitely a more feasible choice. Contrary to what we think, companies in America are relatively free to hire and fire, and employees are quite passionate about their work. Employees respect employers and are friendly towards customers. From a business owner's standpoint, I am also more comfortable with American employees than employees with an oriental mindset, who are often liable to change and act emotionally.

Above all, however, the greatest advantage of entering the US market is being able to take on the entire world once we have captured the US market. This stems from the unique characteristics of the US franchise industry. Business models that have succeeded in the US market have consistent standards that can be applied across the world. There is immense strategic significance in entering other countries using these standards. This can be symbolically illustrated by the overseas export strategies of Daewoo Motors and Hyundai Motor Company. While Daewoo – which wasn't confident of taking on the United States in the finished vehicles market – was operating and developing its East European market, Hyundai attacked the largest market in North America head-on, and grew its business capabilities and product quality. Hyundai became an international finished vehicles company after achieving success in the US market, but Daewoo remained an obscure automobile company that operated on the periphery before meeting its end.

I hope South Korean franchises will bring with them the know-how and capabilities they have acquired thus far, take over the US market, and grow into international brands. This is one of the few opportunities for franchise owners to transform their businesses into international conglomerates. I believe they are fully capable. There will always be an answer if we think of selling great food, instead of patriotism hidden in ginseng chicken soup or *bibimbap*. It won't be too late to enter China twenty years from now. Conversely, this industry is a tomb for early entrants. I hope you won't hurt your own feelings and lose your money by needlessly flocking to China prematurely, and will nurture bigger dreams for the world by introducing Korean food to the US market.

Part 3
Sell What They Want

I establish businesses, preserve family relationships, achieve dreams and make friends by thinking. When I come up with something I wish to achieve or have, I obtain it by imagining and thinking continuously about it. Thoughts and imaginings contain physical power. The instant I think of something, the thought contains physical energy and prepares to manifest itself. This thought makes its first physical appearance when the person who conceived it writes it down on paper. The thought that has been written on paper is real. It's visible and exists independently. I have obtained everything in my life using this simple method.

27
The Power of a CEO

After attending a store opening event, I was on my way out for a simple lunch when I saw that a young mother who had been hired at our store that day was also carrying her lunch. She was pacing up and down looking for a vacant seat, so I suggested we sit together. It must had been awkward and discomfiting that the CEO had suggested to a young, newly hired employee that they eat lunch together. But it was unavoidable, as the only vacant seat was the one in front of me. However, the woman had barely taken a mouthful of her lunch when she suddenly began to cry. Many Americans around us started to cast suspicious glances, presuming that I had scolded the employee.

After I waited a little while, the woman apologised and talked about her past. She and her husband had had a rather large Japanese restaurant, but now it had foundered, they had divorced, and she had to work and raise two children. Her friends were caring for her children so she could work. She cried and asked to run a franchise store. She said if she got a store, she would reconcile with her husband and live her life in earnest, and she requested my help.

I am always at a loss when I receive such requests. No doubt I have the power to accede to them. I feel proud and discomfited that I have this power. I feel proud because I have the power to change someone's life whenever

I want, and discomfited because I fear I might lose this power if I were to exercise it in this manner.

When I look at our employees and their children, I am astonished that the power I have can impact the lives of the children as much as their parents. The reason is that a child's entire life can change when I dismiss or promote someone. No one would complain even if I seized all the company's profits. I risked my family and everything I had when I first started this company, and I have succeeded. Any reward is therefore a reasonable recompense for my hard work. No one contests this, legally or socially. I am omnipotent in the company.

But why didn't I help this woman? Even though she complimented me with a tear-stained face, saying 'Boss, you look different from the others', I could only offer her general advice as calmly as possible. I said, 'Now work hard in this store, and show that you have good rapport with customers. And inform the branch manager of your intention to run a store when a new one comes along, just as you are telling me now. If you prove to be conscientious, the branch manager here will look for you, even without a word from me.'

If I had called the branch manager there and then and instructed him to give this woman a store, I am sure she would talk about me until she grew old, because a dramatic thing had happened to her. However, if that had happened, clearly the core of the allocated schedules – which brand managers carry out according to the company's standards and schedule – would be shaken, and branch managers too would modify the allocated schedules based on their personal standards. If all branch managers did that, the company would be filled with people who would have the right to allocate stores, resort to trickery and serve one another's interests. It's obvious how this company would look many years later.

Even now, my younger brother is operating a franchise store, but I don't participate in the allocation of stores. He may be the CEO's brother, but the employees who oversee store allocation haven't allocated him a good store.

'Now work hard in this store, and show that you have good rapport with customers. And inform the branch manager of your intention to run a store when a new one comes along, just as you are telling me now. If you prove to be conscientious, the branch manager here will look for you, even without a word from me.'

This is because he hasn't yet demonstrated the ability to operate a good store. I can't call the employees and ask them to pay him attention because he is my brother and has three children, including one who is going to college. I want them to give my brother the best store, but for now I am simply waiting eagerly till he shows our employees his ability to operate such a store.

I didn't share my brother's story with this woman, who might have been upset that I hadn't offered direct help. But I feel proud – and at the same time sorry for my brother – when I sometimes hear our employees say that they could be allocated considerably better stores if they did better than the CEO's brother.

You must know that even if you are a CEO who owns one hundred percent of a company's shares, your power comes from the ground up. If you disregard the power that comes from the ground up, and if you disregard popular opinion, this power will someday cease to exist. It's possible for power to gain more power by not exercising it.

A mother who was raising her children without her husband brought a crumpled four-dollar note to a small shop in a corner of the neighbourhood to buy milk powder. When she brought a can of milk powder to the cash register, the shop owner said it cost $7.69. As the mother turned away dejectedly, the shop owner returned the can of milk powder to its place. Then she furtively dropped the can. The shop owner stopped the mother and said the dented can of milk powder was half price. The shop owner received $4 and gave the mother twenty cents in change. The mother obtained the milk powder without wounding her pride, and the shop owner received a piece of heaven for $3.80. It was a wonderful transaction.

Extract from *Note on Self-Management*

28

I Am Therefore a Thinker

When I am passing through airports or filling in hospital medical cards, there are times when I hesitate to write my occupation in the 'occupation' field. I now own a company that has become one of the world's largest bento box distribution chains. But I haven't been involved in managing it for some time. I am also the board chairman of a company that manages financial capital and assets of high-net-worth individuals, but I don't do any actual work. I am a major shareholder at a listed company, but I don't report to work there either. Although I carry several business cards, there is something equivocal about writing down my occupation.

Entrepreneur, businessman, capitalist – they seem more like occupational categories than occupations. It feels odd to call them my occupations. Therefore, when someone on a plane or at a social gathering asks what my occupation is, I simply tell them I am a farmer. It isn't exactly wrong.

This is because I have always liked planting and growing things, I can skilfully memorise the names of the various wild herbs growing in the field, and I am adept at distinguishing the edible ones. If I introduce myself as a farmer, everyone accepts it without asking further. However, if someone seriously asks what I do, I tell them I am a thinker.

Thinkers are people who sustain their livelihoods by specialising in thinking, like solicitors and doctors who make a living by specialising in offering legal advice or treating diseases. I am therefore a thinker.

I establish businesses, preserve family relationships, achieve dreams and make friends by thinking. When I come up with something I wish to achieve or have, I obtain it by imagining and thinking continuously about it.

Thoughts and imaginings contain physical power. The instant I think of something, the thought contains physical energy and prepares to manifest itself. This thought makes its first physical appearance when the person who conceived it writes it down on paper. The thought that has been written on paper is real. It's visible and exists independently. Now a seed has emerged from this thought. And whether this seed of thought will truly manifest itself depends on how long the thought can be sustained. Even if you plant a seed in a flowerpot, it will wither and die right away if you don't water it. When you think constantly so that the seed can grow, your thoughts gradually mature and become a reality that encircles you. I have obtained everything in my life using this simple method.

Previously, an article appeared in which a reporter, after an interview with me, wrongly calculated my sales and assets, valuing my assets at $60 million. I tried to correct this figure through various means, as this amount of assets was non-existent back then, but I heard that I was being needlessly inflexible. It was inevitable, as the figure had already been printed in a book and article.

'I can't correct it. Then I should just become a wealthy man who is worth $60 million,' I told myself. I added to my list of imaginings the dream of becoming a wealthy man who was worth more than $60 million, and now I am no longer embarrassed by that number.

I also gain a sense of connectedness with my wife, children and friends through my imaginings and thoughts. I have achieved the businesses or asset types that I want by first imagining and thinking incessantly about them. Even now, I have more than twenty lists of imaginings. Every year I erase the goals that have been achieved and write new goals in the blank spaces. And I stash the lists in my notebook and look over them when I can. For truly urgent goals, I turn them into email passwords, and this inevitably causes me to think of them three or four times a day. Some imaginings come true in just a few months. But some have taken four years. Some goals ripen in a few months like Korean melons, but some require a longer time because they are like apple trees.

I have shared this method of mine multiple times with people close to me and young people who long to be successful, but it isn't something that can be easily adhered to. This is because they already have other occupations before embarking on their career as thinkers. But there is one thing they don't know: the fact that they don't need to have money, or to show up at another company, to work as thinkers. How much time do we actually need to quietly and constantly repeat our imaginings in our minds at convenient times, unbeknownst to others?

I have obtained everything that others are envious of by investing just a few minutes a day. I am not someone who saved my country in a previous life.[8] I am simply creating a world of my own in my present life.

Now close this book and write down your goals on the back of your business card. Fill up the card. And read it every morning. Look at it until you achieve them. This path is considerably faster and wiser than hoping to win the lottery and buying a ticket every week.

One day, while I was watching TV with my wife, we heard that the first prize in the lottery that night was $18 million. I made a bet with my wife. Would it be faster to earn it? Or faster to win the lottery? Of course, I bet on 'faster to earn it'. It was a bold bet then, when I had only a few employees. I promptly added the goal of $18 million's worth of cash assets to my list of imaginings. Now, three years later, the value of my business has exceeded

---

8   Translator's note: 'Someone who saved the country in a previous life' is a Korean idiom that attributes a person's achievements in their present life to noble work they did in a previous life.

millions of dollars. My wife has already given up buying lottery tickets, and I am using the money to acquire shares in listed companies.

I want to make clear, once again, the secret to becoming a millionaire. Now close this book and write down your goals on the back of your business card. Fill up the card. And read it every morning. Look at it until you achieve them.

29

Travelling with American Entrepreneurs

I was walking with eight American men and women in the night-time streets of Tokyo, Japan. The cherry blossoms, which had come out charmingly at just the right time, yielded to the wind and flew around like snowflakes. It was mid-April 2012, and a quintessentially Japanese beauty. We congregated like teenagers, laughed, chatted, played pranks and amused ourselves. Gathering at the famous Gonpachi restaurant, a three-storey wooden building with a large hall in the centre, we ordered *sake* and Japanese beer, talked about our family photos and children, chatted about the neighbourhoods where we had grown up, and hung out till late at night. We translated into English the slogan the Gonpachi employees shouted, yelled it together, teased the guests seated at the table beside ours, and had a nice time.

As the evening was drawing to a close, I was searching for my shoes to visit the toilet when I saw that our shoes had been arranged side by side under the wooden floor. As only the backs of our shoes could be seen, I had to pull them out one by one to find mine. After rummaging through the shoes, I pulled out the trainers and women's shoes our group had worn. There were no so-called luxury brands among them. They were low- and mid-priced shoe brands commonly seen in ordinary stores. My pair of Calvin

Klein shoes, which had cost $99, appeared to be the costliest. No one can tell who these eight people are by looking at their shoes.

Kikkoman Corporation, then the world's best soy sauce manufacturer, had been hosting various American entrepreneurs every year, to deepen its exchanges with famous entrepreneurs, improve the company's image, and increase its product sales. I too had received an invitation and had wondered whether to participate, as I had a busy schedule and had already visited Japan several times. But I changed my mind once I knew who the other invitees were.

As a Chinese American, Andrew had followed his chef father, travelled through Japan and migrated to America. After founding a restaurant forty years ago at the age of twenty-five, he was now the chairman of Panda Express, which owned one thousand five hundred stores in America. He had also recently played a leading role in shaking up the Korean dry-cleaning business in California by entering the industry through a collaboration with the laundry detergent brand Tide.

Phil, who had come with his wife, looked like a senior university student, but he was the CEO of Stir Foods. He looked too young to be operating a famous company that manufactured and supplied food ingredients, but he laughed and said he too was now forty. I had thought I was the youngest here, but Phil was the youngest.

Jack Link's is a renowned beef jerky company. They produce my favourite beef jerky. It has the softest meat, and one of their seasonings is remarkably and deliciously spicy. If Jack had grown up looking the way he did when he was young, he would still have been the unpopular, physically huge and slow-witted boy from high school. Female classmates who sneered at him then are probably now stamping their feet with regret. Jack Link's beef jerky has grown to become the most successful and famous product in the United States, and can be found at every rural petrol station. Aside from these guys,

CEOs and senior executives of leading companies such as Pei Wei, Wendy's and Heinz Ketchup were also participating. I spent a week with them.

Come to think of it, I had noticed something odd when we first greeted one another at the airport before spending the next few days together. It was an entirely different experience from meeting with South Korean entrepreneurs. If this group had consisted of South Korean entrepreneurs, I would have discovered over the previous few days all about how large their businesses were, how many employees they had, what they had done to make a large profit in one go, where they had purchased land, and where they owned buildings. And above all, I would certainly have grown bored of golf stories I could barely comprehend. For the first two days we shared personal family stories after briefly introducing ourselves and the companies we worked at, and apart from that we didn't share much about our businesses.

On the third day we were visited by Keito, Kikkoman's president for the Americas region, who had joined us belatedly. We exchanged business cards with Keito and then among ourselves as well, and only then did we identify ourselves. But we had already got to know one another through the conversations we had had over the past few days. One David had nine children, and the other David's son was a hero on YouTube because of his Elvis Presley dancing; Sharin danced with style despite being in her early sixties, and it was a fact that she loved *sake*; William had confessed that he owned a three-million-square-foot winery after he happened to recognise the wine on the table during a meal, and then he had collected all of our business cards and said with a swagger that he would send us a box of wine each.

When his promise to send us free wine drew cheers from us, he said the pride of his farm wasn't the wine but the guesthouse, and that we could stay as long as we wanted when we visited. It seemed he had been drinking. Like a drug dealer, he laughed and said the wine was free at first, but we would need to pay for it from the following year onwards. No one in our group boasted about the scale of their business or requested silent investments for new businesses. We simply set aside our computers and emails – something we hadn't done in a long while – and enjoyed ourselves in comfort, thanks to the free trip arranged by Kikkoman.

I suppose they behave like powerful monarchs in their own companies, which have at least several hundred and up to several thousand employees, and that they are very used to receiving respectful treatment. But it was ridiculous even to think that would happen when they stepped out into ordinary society. They were perfectly unpretentious and ordinary people, merely wealthy individuals. They showed me that being wealthy is just one of the various talents a person can have, and it doesn't mean everything to a person.

I have been a CEO throughout my life, without ever drawing a salary from others. After having succeeded and failed repeatedly, I am now building up my company as a mid-sized business, and it's growing rapidly and slowly making its name. Most Americans would know the names of the other participants' companies – unlike mine – and the participants are in a position where their businesses have progressed to full maturity. I am glad I didn't boast to people like them, with the peculiar South Korean swagger, that I would surpass Pei Wei once I had opened all the stores that were scheduled to open this year, and that next year or the year after I would surpass Andrew's Panda Express, a kingdom he had taken forty years to build. It's ludicrous that prior to my trip with these distinguished entrepreneurs I had deliberated over whether to don luxury shoes and put on a watch so as not to lose out to them, at least in attire.

30

Penetrating a $500 Million Market with Three Words

On 27 April 2012, I was inspecting a newly opened store in a city near Phoenix, Arizona.

'Are you Jim Kim?'

An unfamiliar middle-aged couple asked this as they stood behind me. I was about to pace around the newly opened store incognito. Startled, I replied, 'Yes, that is right. How do you know me?'

The middle-aged American couple said they had thought so and told me what they had said between themselves, then gladly extended their hands to shake mine. They said my behaviour had resembled that of a CEO who was monitoring his employees. They were half right. Because I wasn't monitoring our employees, but silently observing the responses of customers in the new store, hiding myself because the employees might feel pressured if I were to appear. I was there for several days, as I was hugely curious as to whether customers in this store would show the same patterns of buying behaviour as customers in ordinary supermarkets, and whether the projected sales from the six menus would pan out normally.

The reason this couple, who were complete strangers, had recognised me in Maricopa, an upper-class city near Phoenix in the state of Arizona, was that they had seen our company's signboard, which was inscribed with my name and had been put up when I was acquiring a local business. 'Wow! How did you establish such a large company and business? I am envious. How many such stores do you have? Isn't it hard operating this business?' they asked. I wondered if they were envious and curious, asking successive questions before even listening to my replies, because they operated a business too.

To answer this couple's questions, I had to go back to three years before. Our company's sales structure then was overly focused on one company – Kroger. As we relied on them for more than eighty percent of our sales, we could never lower our guard, although we were faring well. We needed to diversify our partners urgently. At that time, as a mass merchandiser with warehouses and founded on a membership system, Kroger had piggybacked on favourable reviews from customers for their good-quality products, and had shaken their competitors while keeping up with the speed of progress. It was hugely impressive that they had dominated the market by focusing on product quality and areas where ordinary white middle- and upper-class families lived.

In 2011, Kroger achieved annual sales of $80 billion from hundreds of stores in the United States, and substantially enlarged their market share. They boasted of a colossal sales power that made six to ten times more sales than average food stores. In their city centre stores every product was displayed as if in a 'golden zone', with simple facilities and clear aisles.[9] They were also a company where product quality took precedence, but the image of low prices – in other words, the perception that good-quality products could be purchased cheaply – had been established among customers, and consumers' buying power was strong. In short, the perception that shopping in their stores was a gain had been deeply impressed upon consumers.

---

9   Translator's note: The 'golden zone' is a place on a shelf between chest and shoulder height, where it is most convenient to view and take items.

With their outlet locations, scale of operations and customer base, the bento box market was a perfect blue ocean. There was no other market like it that could diversify our company's sales. My mouth watered. I became truly greedy.

When I calculated the sales of the fresh bento boxes that we could supply to every Kroger's store, there were insufficient zeroes on the calculator I used at home. It amounted to at least three hundred billion Korean won ($300 million). Our sales estimation method had become more elaborate over time and could project up to ninety percent of sales in a region or a store.

I started to feel confident that our projected sales were accurate in 2011, when we achieved sales in our Carrefour stores in France that were consistent with sales from similar stores. The sales of electronic products had surpassed the sales of other products, and although our products had captured a slightly lower percentage of total sales, we were surprised that it tallied with our projected sales, and we couldn't repress our greed. But that was a time when frozen products still dominated stores. Although fresh products were being supplied to ordinary food stores, and demand for frozen products had been falling, there were no buyers who could actualise the idea of directly making and selling food products in warehouse supermarkets, considering the trajectory of food stores in supermarkets then.

I concluded that the bento box market would shift from a market for frozen products to one for fresh products. As resistance to frozen products gradually grew, I was confident that buyers who couldn't withstand the demand for fresh products would call us someday, and it all depended on telling others about us so they would recall our name. And what we could also do was to stop by nearby stores on our way to work every day, recite our 'magic spell', and wipe our drool.

One day, after two years had passed, I heard a strange rumour. Our company couldn't yet get through the door at Costco, as we were still little known, but there were rumours that a small company was hosting a roadshow in their outlet. All fired up, I called our marketing manager, who had just joined us and was then undergoing training, and assigned him his first task.

'Your first task is to reduce our dependence on Kroger. Go and ask Costco.' I had chosen this employee, who had joined us barely a month before, to bag this heavyweight company. The first thing I taught him was to think up our marketing phraseology.

Costco had been operating in six regions across the United States, and each region then operated independently. A few divisions couldn't withstand the demand for fresh products and had tried to work with local chefs and restaurant owners to produce them, but they had failed every time. Their ultimate plan was to supply the products from their factories daily. They planned to turn frozen products with one-week expiry dates into products with two-day expiry dates.

We first defined the word 'fresh' on our own terms. According to our definition, only products that are produced in front of our customers in our stores could be called fresh products. This was purely our own definition. We ourselves decided that products received by delivery and factory-made products couldn't be called fresh products. It was similar to the logic by which only the wine produced in a certain region can be called Champagne, even if other places produce the same wine. We also dubbed our business a 'show business' rather than a food business. The reason was that it was a show to present the direct production of food, and we were confident this could prove the freshness of our products and help customers recall product images. And we named the company, with its system for producing food in front of customers, a 'full-service bento box company'. I gave Joel Stark this phraseology to define our products, services and business, and ordered him to go and hunt Costco down.

Stark was a retired American commissioned officer who had served as a spokesperson for the US Air Force. He couldn't find a proper job after retiring from the services because of the recession, so he moved between jobs as a substitute teacher and grocery cashier, and he sang in a band on the weekends, all the while raising a son as a divorcee. One day, an executive from our company stopped by the grocery shop, saw him hard at work, and invited him for a job interview, and he passed the interview squarely and started working with us. He was a middle-aged man who laughed and talked a lot. He was a gifted conversationalist and proficient in Korean, as he had previously also worked in South Korea.

Costco, which had been indifferent to us three years before, crumbled helplessly in the face of altered market conditions, Stark's smooth talking, and the words and sentences we had devised. In less than a month we held consecutive meetings, and in the following month we produced and presented food samples, registered our business, entered our barcodes, and agreed to open stores in their outlets. Everything had unfolded with lightning speed.

In particular, the power of our new phraseology was formidable.

'Does your company offer fresh bento boxes?' Stark asked them.

They said yes. Stark asked again, as he had been trained to.

'Are your so-called fresh bento boxes delivered from factories? If that is the case, you can't call them fresh.'

They explained that the bento boxes were delivered every morning and were quite different from the factory-made bento boxes sold previously. Stark thrust in a sharper knife.

'But are the consumers aware of that?'

They hesitated to respond.

'You can't call them fresh products, no matter where they are delivered from. You should restrict "fresh products" to products that are made in front of customers, and call them as such.'

They began to crumble.

'If that is the case, what do you guys want to do?'

Now they were asking us. We explained the full-service bento box system. And we explained the fact that this was show business. Once we gave all the information and statistics to show that this business method could maximise sales, they too started to comprehend our business. A few distinct words opened their eyes. And they wanted to put us to the test to see if we were bluffing. After they had surveyed several of our stores that had been selected as test sites, they learned that projected monthly sales for a 142-square-foot store ranged between as much as $200,000 and $300,000. This figure was so massive that even our employees found it unbelievable. This sales volume was impossible, even for exclusive stores like those in casinos or airports. If there were only one airport that could achieve this sales volume, any company would jump at it as if it were a matter of life and death, but Costco had hundreds of such stores. Of course, they didn't know that.

I persuaded our employees, who had always been slightly doubtful, and instructed them to procure staff and supplies to meet a monthly sales target of $200,000 for our newly opened store in Maricopa, which had been selected as the first test store. Our counterparts thought it would be a jackpot if we made $40,000, but once our goal had been revealed through an employee's blunder, they too rattled on about our goal and tried to claim credit for it. It didn't matter to us. It was evident that we would achieve enormous sales, and we knew that we would rise at a stroke to become number one in the American business world, starting with this store. Getting ready for the store opening was like fighting a war. All the employees who had been working in shirts and ties in the office donned chef's uniforms and, together with sixteen temporary workers, produced our products all day long, from three in the morning till late at night.

Our customers snapped up our products as if they had been waiting for this day. No matter how many products our many employees produced, there was no end to production. When we could no longer cope using the display stands we had prepared, we cleared additional spaces in the store to place more display stands. We produced sushi for six hundred to a thousand people each day. One in seven customers snapped up the sushi, which consistently accounted for 1.2 percent of Costco's total sales daily. It was a huge success. After the first week, sales stood at $40,173. This figure was the highest for any bento boxes sold in American supermarkets. As far as I knew, it was the highest sales figure among individual bento box stores in supermarkets around the world. Two days later, Costco's person in charge flew over from California and could barely contain his exhilaration. Besides the presidents of other divisions, their CEO also visited us, handed out his business card, and wanted us to promise him that we would contact him.

*

I was delightedly watching the crowd while trying to remain incognito and steer clear of employees who might feel pressured by having me around the store for a couple of days. Some customers saw me at the back of the store, guessed who I was, and asked again.

'Are you Jim Kim?'

It was an elderly woman this time.

'Yes. How did you know?'

'There is a way to find out,' she laughed.

Detained by this elderly woman, I stepped out of the store, leaving behind the process by which the single word 'fresh' had morphed into a business worth hundreds of millions of dollars. I left the store with her to hear the story of this elderly woman, a former entrepreneur who was spending her vacation and enjoying her life after handing her business over to her son.

'Well, how did you start this company?' she asked as we were walking. 'I did everything I could to sell candles here. What is your secret? I want to teach my son.'

As I looked into her enquiring eyes, I wasn't confident about telling her that 'all I did was redefine three phrases', so I said I was simply fortunate. I wasn't wrong either. In our company – which has grown into a wonderful

'It didn't matter to us. It was evident that we would achieve enormous sales, and we knew that we would rise at a stroke to become number one in the American business world, starting with this store.'

mid-sized corporation because of good employees, competent chefs, changes in food culture, and powerful sales networks – all I did was to contribute three phrases – 'fresh', 'show business' and 'full service' – as weaponry, and send Stark on his mission. If you aspire to start a new business, I just want to inform you how important it is to first define your business phraseology, and to adopt it before others do.

Those who can fly should help those who walk rather than remove their wings, so that both can fly together. Once a fishing expedition ends, a ship owner decides on the shares, and divides the fish among the captain and crew based on their roles. The shares differ, but when the ship returns loaded with fish, the whole pie becomes larger, and the distributed shares grow bigger too. I hope employees will receive more dividends than salary. Greed is the only ageless passion. I hope employees will make use of me and an appropriate degree of greed and work passionately, as if operating their own businesses.

Extract from *The Kimbap CEO*

31

Guardhouse, Toilets, CEO's Office and Stakeholder Policy

Over the past two years, I have been buying stocks in Uno & Company, a South Korean listed company that manufactures and exports fibre wigs to the United States. Despite good capital strength and technology, this company is intriguingly undervalued when one inspects its accounts. I decided to visit the company personally. I have peculiar criteria for evaluating whether a company that has been assessed numerically actually has value.

When I visit a company to decide whether I should buy stocks in it, there are two locations I will certainly stop by before visiting the CEO's office. The guardhouse and toilets. It's easiest to find out whether the volume of goods and number of employees have increased over the past year by sitting in the guardhouse, sharing a cup of coffee. I can also find out whether the CEO comes to work regularly, and whether the top brass are working conscientiously. If it's a growing company, its energy can best be felt from the guardhouse. But this company didn't have a guardhouse. Then the second place I visit is the toilets. Toilets are the last department managed by a company. If the toilets are squalid, it shows that the company is currently not being properly governed. Toilets where toilet paper is strewn on the floor, the taps are filthy, and the mirrors are covered with soap bubbles are a realistic portrayal of how the company is currently being managed. Toilets are never squalid in an organisation where the business system is reliable, rules and regulations are well observed, and employees work conscientiously.

The toilets in this company were immaculate. The towels on the wall were neat and clean, and I could tell that the toilets were being maintained hourly. Just by looking at the toilets, I could deduce how credible the annual business reports presented by this company were.

The last place I visit is the CEO's office. The CEO's office is where I can assess the proclivities of the company's representative. CEOs who love to show off and are keener on activities outside their businesses will naturally fill their walls with commendation certificates, appointment letters, medals, commemorative plaques, appreciation plaques and so on. If these don't suffice, there will be an array of items on their desk. And a golf club will be leaning in one corner on a thick carpet. These people have multiple business cards and diverse job titles. They hold titles as board directors or presidents of alumni associations or other associations.

I have a simple reason for adopting this childish method as a yardstick for deciding whether to invest in a company. I am not a mere a stock investor. I have no interest in making money through speculative means by aligning with short-term increases in stock prices. This is because any money I have made by these means has always tended to disappear more easily. I buy stocks because I wish to own the company in question. And owning a company is possible only by buying their stocks on the stock market. People visit a bistro and inspect its inventory and the condition of its facilities when they decide to acquire it, but when they buy stocks they only read news articles and instantly rush to their monitors. They listen only to descriptions, and buy the box without knowing what's inside the wrapping paper. That is speculating, not investing.

I was fortunate. The CEO of this company I had visited was unreservedly easy-going. The carpet wasn't thick, there were no plaques for him to show off with, and the walls were adorned with product samples. He was a typical CEO who loved his work. I was heartened when an employee who was present said, 'Our CEO never fails to return his remaining travel allowance after his business trips.' What more could I ask for if he was such a gentleman?

After visiting the company, I continued to increase my shares through the stock market, and soon became the largest shareholder after several official notices. I was neither disappointed nor terrified when the stock price didn't rise as expected. I simply thought there was plenty of time left to become closely acquainted with this girl who would become a ravishing beauty in time to come, and for her to address me as an older brother. There was no change in the inherent value of the company. I was observing in a leisurely way, like an old friend, because I knew the day would come when this company would receive a proper evaluation.

But the market didn't think likewise. My actions were constantly suspected of laying the groundwork for a hostile takeover of a South Korean company by foreign capital. Since before the shareholders' meeting in 2014, the plans of many major shareholders, who owned significantly more shares than company executives, had been cast in the spotlight. They were mentioned in the same breath as the management rights dispute at Shinil Industrial, and speculative articles had started to do the rounds. On my way back along the expressway after the shareholders' meeting, I browsed the Internet and found that articles written by reporters who hadn't even attended the meeting had already been uploaded in the meantime. Perhaps releasing the official notice that I would be participating in company management had become a curse. My reason for getting involved in company management stemmed from my objective of 'business cooperation' rather than to exercise a major shareholder's inalienable right to interfere. But this intention of mine wasn't recognised, because most major shareholders on South Korea's stock market participated in management with the intention of taking over the management rights.

I am a businessman in America. According to what I have been taught, shareholders are the owners of a company. The company's representative isn't the owner. It's akin to saying that the owners of a country aren't the political leaders, but the people themselves. Even if I own ninety-nine percent and my friend owns one percent of the shares, I can't use the company card for my personal expenses. This is because one percent of it isn't my money. The word 'corporation' itself suggests that shareholders are company owners.[10] Of course, this is something company executives must embrace if they want to offer shares for public subscription and list their companies. But there are many instances where numerous South Korean executives have perceived shareholders as vagabonds who are borrowing money without interest. There have also been occasions where short-term investors in particular aren't even recognised as shareholders. However, even short-term investors are company owners – no less so than those who have owned long-standing shares since the day the company was founded. The same goes without saying for long-term investors.

I wanted to get the representatives of companies listed on South Korea's stock market interested in a rational 'shareholder policy'. I had publicly announced my participation in management to convey the clear message that 'you run the business, but you work for the shareholders', but I was still regarded dubiously within the company and by business reporters. I might need to quietly wait a tad longer if my peculiar message was to gain credibility. Fortunately, I have slowly broadened my understanding with Uno & Company, and despite the recession we have distributed several rounds of cash surpluses and are working towards boosting dividends and stock prices – as our shareholders wish – through a shares buyback.

---

10 Translator's note: The Korean word for 'corporation' is *jushikhoesa* (주식회사), the first two characters of which mean 'shares'. This implies that shareholders – people who own shares in a company – are the owners of the company.

It's my dream and request that people in all positions – politicians and entrepreneurs – who assume the rights of many people and exert power over them will use their decisions for the good of the public and the members of their organisations. Even powerless and vulnerable citizens, and minority shareholders who work diligently and save their tiny salaries to purchase just a handful of shares, are citizens and shareholders too. My voting rights will be used to find and employ such politicians, and I want to use my shares to find and help executives who use their decisions for the good of the public and their organisations. I say this because I find it regrettable that this natural request is always regarded with suspicion.

32

The Right-Behind-Person Strategy

There are two broad reasons for starting a specific business. We start a business because we look around us and think that certain items seem to be selling well these days, or because we think they may sell well in the future. The first reason looks relatively reliable, but there are numerous occasions when competition suddenly intensifies, earnings fall, and businesses board the last train and disappear downhill. With the second reason, the most adventurous businesses will take the lead in the industry, and it's a big win for them when they succeed, but the majority of businesses will be left battered and bruised. Both approaches are risky. But there is a way to distribute the risks. This is called the right-behind-person strategy.

Sometimes, when we watch hunting shows where foragers are ploughing through a dense forest and moving in a group to gather fruit, the person at the very front wields a machete as they lead the way. The person at the front has courage and strong intuitive judgement. They predict places where there will be food, then open a way ahead. But their entire body is bruised. They can't find a single fruit because they are looking out for poisonous plants, snakes and venomous insects. The person who follows right behind is more relaxed, and they survey their surroundings and find edible fruit. The third person has nothing to eat, contrary to expectation, because the person in front of them has taken all the fruit.

The first person, who wields the jungle machete, is usually a trailblazer. They are highly intelligent and a doer. They aren't afraid of predicting their own future and blazing a trail. There are a few reasons why these people vanish from the business world despite their intelligence. The first reason is capital strength. They enter a dense forest without proper equipment. Their shoes aren't sturdy enough to withstand snakes' fangs, and their skin, exposed by shorts and short-sleeved shirts, is slashed by sharp leaves. They don't have enough water and can't overcome thirst. They have insufficient capital, but they are unable to imagine how far they are from their destination, because their faith in their new idea is too strong. The other reason is that it's premature for the market to embrace their idea. It's as if it's spring and the flowers are in bloom, but one looks at the flowers and thinks there will be summer fruit soon.

If the failure of the person in front is an idea backed by insufficient capital and market prematurity, the idea is always worth undertaking nevertheless. Even if the person in front has succeeded, the 'right-behind-person strategy' is still very useful. This is because the person right behind can benefit if the person in front has small pockets or too much fruit. The truth is there are very few businesses in the real world that are started anew and on an enormous scale based on powerful capital strength and information. Today's conglomerates and most thriving businesses have grown by wisely applying the 'right-behind-person strategy'. Most individuals and small businesses have hauled enormous baskets or trucks and followed behind while someone else wields a jungle machete.

I fought fearful prejudice to sell bento boxes in American supermarkets initially, and I treaded on the heels of companies that had forged ahead but suffered defeat before I established my present business. These companies had fought with sandwich companies every morning to place one more bento box on the display stands, and had clashed with the market over aversion to food that contained raw fish, before they disappeared altogether. Fortunately,

I was standing right behind them. Our company had captured no market share, although we were only two years late in joining the industry. The reason is that back then, local restaurant owners too were relaxed enough to take up this business idea, but now only companies with nationwide systems can survive, and it's no longer possible to enter the market.

In sports we remember only the victor. Second or third place is no different from sixteenth place. However, unlike in sports events, the one who survives in business is the victor. The survivor takes first place. Therefore, I hope we won't blame ourselves for not having the keen insights of a trailblazer, but that we acquire the ability of a second-in-place person to identify trailblazers.

33

Frontier Uprising or City Revolution

You are now living in Later Han dynasty China, around 200 AD. And let's presume that you have decided to establish a new nation and become king. You have a cause and have assembled your comrades.

Now there are two tactical methods to become king. One method is to amass power on the frontier, unbeknown to the current king, and gradually enlarge your territory, then launch a full-fledged war and conquer the nation once you have a cause and sufficient support to withstand government forces. The other method is to start a revolution one day, unexpectedly, in the capital where the king lives, and seize power overnight. The former case, occupying the capital thanks to an uprising on the frontier, is a method used by new powerholders with weak influence. The latter case, plotting a revolution in the capital, is a method used by power holders who are already at the centre of power.

It's similar with business. Entrepreneurs without capital must first firmly secure their position in the countryside or suburbs in order to enter and compete within an existing business paradigm that is unfolding vigorously. They then move into city centres such as Gangnam in Seoul or Manhattan in New York. Conversely, innovative new businesses with ample capital succeed in the very centre of the city before expanding to satellite cities and provinces.

I started my supermarket bento box business in Houston, in the southern United States, rather than in New York or Los Angeles, where the existing markets were the largest. I launched the world's largest bento box company in a neighbourhood renowned for cowboys. It's the same way Walmart started in Rogers, a small north-western city in the state of Arkansas, before taking over the entire world. Our company took over the entire state of Texas in the first two years from our inception, and industry leaders thought nothing of us even when we were amassing influence. They must have regarded us as little kids from the countryside and ignored us. But we broadened our reach to the state of Michigan at the end of our second year, the state of Oklahoma in the third year, the states of Virginia, California, Arizona and Utah in the fifth year, and we continued to expand to Indiana, Kentucky and Ohio, to the alarm of existing businesses.

Every year we expanded our market to new territories, walked all over existing businesses that had maintained old business methods, and broadened our influence tremendously. Later, in the same way we devoured most European countries, where the bento box industry had been leaderless, and set foot in Australia. Our competitors were put on the defensive, and they either requested a merger or became apprehensive. The uprising on the frontier had succeeded beautifully. Fettered by our company, our competitors are now absorbed in the defence of their own capitals. They are in a situation where they feel grateful simply to preserve their current positions.

This business category began more than twenty years ago and has now entered a growth phase. The current bento box market across the whole United States is worth $1 billion annually. This time I have initiated an internal revolution against the entire industry, which includes our company. Commercial property rents in major city centres today have been rising yearly, irrespective of market conditions. Aside from the flagship stores that conglomerates have opened for promotional purposes, there are barely any businesses that have paid these massive rents and still survived. There are coffee shops that have survived by weaponising relatively high margins and customer turnover rates, but as seen in Tokyo, they can now no longer sustain both.

For two years now, I have been constantly warning people in the industry that coffee shops can no longer survive in South Korea's main commercial districts. This is because the rents in shopping districts have been constantly rising, even though the price of coffee can no longer be marked up. Coffee shops will retreat to secondary commercial districts and be replaced by businesses that offer reasonable prices. Which businesses will then occupy the main commercial districts? Might they be businesses with faster customer turnover rates than coffee shops? I found the answer in London, United Kingdom.

For several years, certain businesses have been moving steadily into London. They aren't restaurants or convenience stores. These businesses have been slowly expanding their territories, even as they pay the world's highest rents in London. Each individual store has been yielding profit. I assigned a new category to this business method in the food distribution industry and started to call it 'grab and go'.

Grab-and-go businesses are restaurants, but they are restaurants that don't take orders. Everything is produced on the spot in front of customers, and then displayed immediately on shelves. It therefore resembles the way products are sold in convenience stores. It's a composite of a restaurant and a convenience store. Customers can take away the finished products that are on display, or simply consume them in the store. Two years ago, our company launched this business model in major cities in the United States. This year we opened dozens of stores in Seoul, Manhattan and other places using the high-density multistore approach, and we are opening additional stores. This is an operation to release into the wild stores that have been growing under the protection of shopping malls and supermarkets.

This operation is an internal revolution for the industry. If the revolution succeeds, the industry will burgeon into a market worth $3 billion a year

'These days our company sells around a hundred thousand bento boxes every day across our stores worldwide. Now we are our own competitor. We aim to sell more than four hundred thousand bento boxes daily, and have already thrown our hat into the ring to become "The World's Largest Grab-and-Go Company".'

in five years' time. And it looks as if our company, which is leading this revolution, will secure additional sales of more than $1 billion through new projects alone. If we can outdistance our competitors, it's possible that we will monopolise seventy percent of market share, worth more than $2 billion. This is an operation to make the uprising on the frontier of the business world a success, and to maintain our position as frontrunner by launching another palace coup in a mature business territory.

Business is sometimes very similar to politics. We must have an external cause, rally our comrades, procure munitions, assemble the generals and train the soldiers. We must understand consumer trends, study the present times, and draw up individual tactics and strategies before going to war. This was what Liu Bei did before he established his own state.[11] We set out on this path ten years ago and grabbed a business category in the food industry.

We have truly become 'The World's Largest Bento Box Company', as we wrote in our office many years ago. These days our company sells around a hundred thousand bento boxes every day across our stores worldwide. Now we are our own competitor. We aim to sell more than four hundred thousand bento boxes daily, and have already thrown our hat into the ring to become 'The World's Largest Grab-and-Go Company'. We have transformed an empire and are enlarging the borders of this transformed empire. Will we go to war with other empires once we have secured our borders? I think so. This is because doing business is like riding a bicycle: we will fall off if there isn't constant forward movement.

---

11 Translator's note: Liu Bei was a warlord during the Later Han dynasty in China. He founded the state of Shu-Han during the Three Kingdoms period, which started after the end of the Han dynasty.

34

What to Look Out for When Your Business Grows

There are experiences that most CEOs will have once their businesses start to find their place and grow, and employees begin to join through open recruitment. It's a natural course for businesses to experience them; they are the mountains that must be crossed to reach the highest peak. I want to inform you beforehand that there will be several gorges and precipices before you reach that peak. Those who have been through this path know this, but numerous individuals have walked this path and suffered distress and injury, and some of them eventually found it unbearable and turned back. These gorges usually appear when the number of employees starts to exceed ten. Ten is the maximum number of employees to whom a CEO can issue orders directly. When the number of employees exceeds ten, there are more people who receive their orders not directly from the CEO but through a manager.

The first gorge is friends. In the early days of our business, our friends cheer us on and encourage us as much as they can. However, as our business gradually grows, and the gap between our friends and us begins to widen, there will be deserters among our friends. They will keep us in check by saying that we have recently become arrogant, that we are domineering because we are doing well, or they will ask us to pay for drinks. This jealousy will come not only from our friends, but from our close family and other relatives too. That said, the fortunate thing is that this jealousy automatically disappears once your business has expanded so much that your friends can no longer envy it. This is because a farmer with a hundred *seom*[12] of rice invites envy, but a farmer with a thousand *seom* of rice receives respect. But the number of friends and relatives who ask for money will continue to increase. Here you should always stay firm. Let's not claim to be penniless. Such words will sound like an excuse to them, and the requests will never cease.

My stand was: 'I can give you money, but I don't lend it.' It didn't matter if they were my siblings, parents or best friends. If it's money that you can simply give away, give it away without any unnecessary remarks. But you need the courage and audacity to never lend. Whether you give or lend, the probability of not getting it back is the same. The only difference is that the sum that the other party receives as a gift will be smaller than if they had asked for a loan, and they will feel embarrassed to ask again. However, the more money you lend under the premise that it will be repaid, and the worse this situation becomes – that is, the higher the probability of not getting the money back – the more likely these loan requests will recur.

The second precipice is the revolt of founding members. In the early days of our business, we start out with our relatives or younger friends in mind. They are people who lack the requisite skills but participate zealously when the owner starts a business. They are people who have undergone considerable hardships, playing multiple roles without demarcating responsibilities, and with whom we have weathered difficulties together. We are of the same mind, and this leads to personal relationships as if between younger siblings and an older brother rather than a superior. The problem begins when the business expands and requires systematic management. A company with

---

12 Translator's note: *Seom* is a traditional Korean unit of measurement for crops. One *seom* is equivalent to 180 litres.

ten employees and a company with thirty employees differ not just three times in number; they are companies that are entirely different in structure.

When the number of employees increases from twenty to thirty, the CEO can no longer run the company by rule of thumb. The CEO therefore feels an acute need to document and specify everything. Furthermore, as the company gradually comes to need professional staff, and the composition of employees shifts towards educated individuals, the standards of the founding members become lower relatively. To make up for this, the founding members pull rank, distort the CEO's orders midway, or assert their authority as founding members by treating other employees with disdain. But there is something founding members are unable to comprehend. The CEO can lead the company without them once the company has already expanded, but the company can't grow bigger without new employees who will work systematically.

The concerns of the CEO snowball, and they eventually arrive at a situation where, for the sake of the entire company, they lay off founding members or refuse them preferential treatment. By then, the founding members think they are being discarded because they are no longer useful, while the CEO fails to comprehend why they are unable to adhere to the system and are burning with jealousy. The CEO feels sorry to dismiss them, and they become the ribs of a strangled chicken[13] if they are retained, but the CEO eventually realises that they can sustain the company only by dismissing them.

Revolt ensues in this situation, and there will be cases of embezzlement or the trading of personal insults. In the end, founding members who are unable to assimilate into the system agree that they should be dismissed. This

---

13 Translator's note: Chicken ribs typically have little meat, and some people find it a pity to discard them. Here the author implies that founding members, like chicken ribs, may have little usefulness, but it may be a pity to dismiss them.

is because new employees politely address the CEO as such and work within the system, but founding members repeatedly address the CEO as an older brother, pop in and out of the office without permission, and even disregard the need to obtain approval. This scenario appears when we examine why when Liu Bei – once an ordinary 'big brother' in the neighbourhood – became king, his younger sworn brother Zhang Fei, who moved the troops as he pleased, reached the point of having to beg Zhuge Liang for his life.[14] The older brother should be served as a king when he becomes one, but he won't be able to lead the organisation if the founding members still consider him an older brother.

If founding members wish to continue growing with the CEO, they must quickly learn how to work within a system and an organisation. But most founding members are destined to journey with the CEO only up to a certain precipice, because they claim credit for setting up the company and find no meaning in sustained progress. Their strongest merit from the CEO's perspective is their sense of loyalty, but if this loyalty isn't backed up by education then it returns as disloyalty. Education is the only solution. When they are asked to undergo professional education and management training, they are the best allies if they accept it, but if they don't, then they must eventually part ways with the company.

The third gorge is extravagance. We are naturally more relaxed once we have established ourselves and our income far outweighs our expenditures. Now the CEO doesn't sweat and can afford to conceive new business ideas or run the company on a simple approval system. They change their car, their

14 Translator's note: Liu Bei was a warlord who established the state of Shu-Han during the Three Kingdoms period in China. Zhang Fei was his sworn brother and a military general who served under him; Zhuge Liang was the chancellor of Shu-Han. After the founding of Shu-Han, Zhang Fei – a founding member of the state – moved the troops without consulting Liu Bei or Zhuge Liang.

house and even their golfing friends. They also go abroad on the pretext of conceiving new business ideas. There is nothing particularly wrong about buying houses and cars with the wealth one has earned. However, the problem snowballs when, for reasons of keeping up appearances, the CEO starts to take out loans under the presumption that their current income will stay unchanged in the future. This habit doesn't disappear even when the business expands. The loan amounts will burgeon, because the house will get larger and the car costlier as the business thrives.

To splurge because of overwork is a behaviour caused by thinking that you are less significant than others, or by a sense of inferiority. There are always people who are wealthier than you, no matter how much you earn. Your sense of inferiority can't be remedied by splurging. There is nothing as impressive as someone who could squander as much as they wished but doesn't do so. Unless they look poverty-stricken.

The fourth precipice is honour. It's human to want to be honoured when we become wealthy. Wealth can simply be earned, but honour can't be obtained easily. However, there are several honours that can be bought with money in the marketplace. They include titles such as president of an alumni association, president of a hometown alumni association, president of alumni from top courses in various universities, president of similar-interest groups, association board member, head of a government-affiliated organisation, and so on. Some people also dream of holding public office. I think it's amusing the way some people amass honour by donating $10,000 or $20,000 a time, receiving palm-sized appreciation plaques one after another, and displaying them in the office in exchange for titles such as class alumni president or former president, and for being addressed as president. On one hand these people are regarded as pushovers, but on the other hand they love juniors who politely address them as 'president'.

People who are somewhat respectable form friendships with renowned individuals, CEOs of larger companies, members of parliament or ministers.

They are under the illusion that they are equal to these individuals, and start to brag when they meet subordinates or friends. From here on, their relationships with their families usually start to break down. Because they are often busy outside, and show little concern for the families that have accompanied them on this arduous path. They say that they are doing this to build connections for their businesses, but contrary to what they say, their businesses begin to lapse. Employees let down their guards at work and think simply of getting paid, because the CEO is more concerned about external matters than business. Good employees start to think of changing jobs. And at this point, an up-and-coming competitor nearly catches up with them.

These things don't bring honour to entrepreneurs. An entrepreneur receives the greatest honour when they start a business as a breadwinner, assume full responsibility for their family's future, and maintain this responsibility to the end, so that their family never again has to experience the insecurity they once did. An entrepreneur is honoured when they pay their employees on time, help each individual grow, and create more jobs for society. Only in doing these things can an entrepreneur receive the greatest honour from their family, employees and society. You must awaken to the fact that appreciation plaques and appointment letters will embarrass you.

The fifth mountain pass is operating a business for self-interest. Only by crossing this precipice can a small business grow into a mid-sized business. If you keep at it, it could also grow into a conglomerate. This fifth precipice is a problem that arises when a business starts to expand beyond a certain scale, to the point where we can no longer memorise every employee's name, and where it begins to yield profits that are comparable to those of listed companies. From then on, executives yearn to be recognised as entrepreneurs among entrepreneurs, rather than to work for their own business. They build office buildings that are larger and offices that are more magnificent than their competitors'. They open branch offices or stores abroad. This is because their desire to demonstrate the company's growth symbolically has taken precedence over the practical benefits of doing so. They undertake barely profitable projects and prioritise them under the pretext of investing, as if they could foresee the future. The addresses of their branch offices in Hong Kong or the United States are engraved on their business cards.

They also give pompous newspaper interviews, as if they could defeat multinational brands in one fell swoop. They appear on magazine covers looking dignified and gentle, with their arms folded. Once the magazines are published, they buy five hundred copies on the pretext of giving them away as gifts, and then keep them for promotional purposes; but there is no one to distribute them to, apart from some family members, and they are piled up in a corner of the warehouse. By now we should see that these executives aren't working for their businesses; they are operating businesses in order to have the upper hand compared with other entrepreneurs, or to brag to friends.

Their ability ends here. Even if their business has been thriving, most of those who often appear in interviews as business owners, or who start a business to show off their abilities, disappear quietly after a few years. Business is very much about reality. In reality, companies disappear when they make just one misstep. Do not operate a business for the sake of appearances or power. This is a path you have walked doggedly, and a business you have worked hard to build.

Only after crossing these gorges, precipices and mountain pass can we achieve a business that will last a generation. A business grows through unending learning and self-awareness. I had to endure poverty, contempt, physical hardship and spot baldness to actualise one business. I can't lose a company that I built up laboriously just because of extravagance or appreciation plaques. I hope you will hang in there a tad longer till you reach the pinnacle.

Reader's Digest

I titled
this picture 'Never Give Up!'
There were times when I, the frog, looked so feeble
and powerless
resisting destiny, the stork.
Still, never give up.
If you think your belief is right,
never give up.
Even if a rough hand called destiny
coils around and strikes the nape of your neck,
never give up.
I hope you will raise
a frog in your heart today.

Extract from *The Kimbap CEO*

35

The Significance of the Fruit Trees in Our Headquarters Garden

There are numerous fruit trees growing at our headquarters in Houston. A small sign is affixed in front of every single fruit tree. Tangerine trees are planted evenly in rows on one side, and grouped in lines and rows on the other side. On tiny signs affixed in front of towering trees are written employees' names, their year of joining the company, and the order in which they joined. On trees that have been grouped separately and planted one at a time, the words 'For those who have believed in and supported our business' are written under the names of key employees from partner companies. They were people who believed in us and gave us work when we were expanding our business, accountants and individuals who lent a helping hand in the early days of our business.

The tangerines growing on our employees' trees are harvested at year's end. After the harvest, our company distributes bonuses to employees based on the size and quantity of the harvested tangerines, then packs and mails the tangerines to employees at our partner companies.

These trees were the very first thing we planted as soon as we bought the office building. Our headquarters employees, as well as employees in branch and overseas offices, each have a tree of their own. Therefore, when they visit headquarters for training or education, they look around to see if their trees are thriving. Headquarters employees too survey their trees during their free time to see if they are thriving. The intriguing thing is that the trees belonging to employees who have resigned bear few fruit, or even shrivel and die. But the trees that belong to employees who have been promoted and recognised in the company are unquestionably sturdy and bear abundant fruit and flowers. It feels as if the individual and their tree are bound by an unknown thread. We joke about whether employees secretly pee on their trees or furtively add fertiliser, but these may not actually be jokes.

In any case, to lavish affection on one's tree is also to lavish affection on the company. Trees that belong to employees who have affection for the company thus grow better than other people's trees. For that reason, paying bonuses according to the size and quantity of the fruit harvested isn't so unreasonable. Above all, though, the beautiful thing is the feeling of a tangible community. It gives members of an organisation a sense of security and belonging if they have a tree of their own whose roots have been planted in their workplace. The trees remain even if they resign. The presence of a single entity that continues to grow and bear fruit in the company creates the most significant sense of unity.

Trees are a symbol. But they are a symbol that exists in reality. As an owner, I detach myself from any sense of personal closeness to each employee. I know full well that most employees won't call on me again once they leave the company. This isn't a matter of affection or loyalty, but the way of life. I am therefore neither despondent nor expectant. I am most delighted if they call on me, and it's expected if they do not. But I think of them, because the trees exist as long as the company is still around, and I believe they too will think of the company or me, at least once, when the fruit is in season.

A new employee, whose name I haven't yet retained, steps out into the garden after lunch, reads the inscriptions on each tree and searches for his tree. As I look at him from afar, I feel the satisfaction of a CEO.

'It gives members of an organisation a sense of security and belonging if they have a tree of their own whose roots have been planted in their workplace. The trees remain even if they resign. The presence of a single entity that continues to grow and bear fruit in the company creates the most significant sense of unity.'

36

Twelve Signs of a Failing Business

If the following scenarios befall a CEO, they are signs that their business is failing. These signs sometimes also appear during an economic boom or when a business is thriving. If there are no such signs when a business is growing or even shrinking, it will likely recover from any setback. But employees should prepare to jump ship when the twelve signs listed below become apparent, because their company is on the classic path to ruin.

1. **When the CEO plans to grow the business by receiving help from politicians or journalists.** A CEO should adopt a 'not too close, not too far' attitude towards politicians and journalists. If the CEO plans to grow the business in one fell swoop at any cost, by relying on unconventional forces, they will eventually destroy the business.

2. **When the number of instructions issued to subordinates or the verification of completed work decrease noticeably.** This is a tremendously grave scenario. It's a scenario in which individuals who are responsible for issuing and enforcing instructions have disappeared.

3. **When employees are often unaware of the CEO's whereabouts.** This is a situation where employees presume the CEO is out meeting women or gambling, or that the business can no longer survive.

4. **When the CEO shows an interest in upper-class hobbies and indulges in paintings, cars, ornamental trees and the like.** There

are very few instances where a CEO aspires to be a refined person rather than an entrepreneur and can preserve both their business and their refinement. When self-made entrepreneurs in particular aspire to this, their businesses won't last two generations.

5. **When the CEO starts to socialise with celebrities, top government officials and politicians, and boasts about it.** The CEO wants to raise their own worth to be on a par with these heavyweights, but they gain nothing compared with what they invest in cultivating such relationships. This is one of the very worst investments.

6. **When the CEO's newly made friends frequent the office without being escorted.** This happens when formal boundaries in the office diminish. The authority of employees isn't respected, and when the number of such friends of the CEO increases, there will also be friends who give orders to the employees.

7. **When the CEO replaces themselves with a professional manager and starts to amass other titles, such as chairman and so on.** It's possible for someone who is more attracted to job titles than business management to return to management only if they have failed once.

8. **When photos of the CEO with their arms folded feature in news articles and magazines, or their media appearances become more frequent.** The more you want to boast to the world about yourself, or to receive flattering calls from former classmates, the higher the possibility that you will end up as someone who used to be successful.

9. **When the CEO looks down on and overtly disregards competitors.** Looking down on your competitors is the same as disparaging the industry you are in. When your affection for the industry dies, your business dies too.

10. **When family members are placed in key positions because they are family, and executive positions are filled with close associates.** When the number of family members and close associates in a

company increases, competent employees will concede defeat beforehand and leave the company. Peculiar animals that have enormous heads but no waists or legs will eventually die.

11. **When the CEO is unable to kick the habit of overeating and binge eating.** These habits ruin our bodies and prevent us from thinking clearly. Our minds that make judgements and our bodies that work will die. Nor will heaven help these people. Because they are living recklessly.

12. **When a CEO's donations surge, and their plaques and appointment letters fill more than one wall.** This happens when a CEO doesn't work for the company but uses the company for their own advancement. At times like this, the company will abandon the CEO.

37

Seven Reasons Why a Kind CEO Fails

First and foremost, a kind CEO desires to be a good person to everyone. But they can't be a good person to everyone. Someone who is good to everyone may also be a person who is bad to everyone. Sometimes we should be cool-headed, act firmly and fight. If we can't be firm when we should, if we can't stay cool-headed when we must, and if we step back when we ought to fight, our closest family, friends and employees will suffer. If you desire to remain a good person to everyone, you shouldn't do business but become the owner of a mountain villa.

Second, a kind CEO doesn't know how to say no. But nothing happens even when they do say no. A kind person believes that the other party will feel insulted or dejected if they say no to them. But most respectful requests are prepared for rejection, and requests suffused with greed will sneer at us even if we hear them out, or will turn back and curse at us. Even saying no requires practice. It isn't a big deal once we learn to say no. Saying no appropriately raises your value instead.

Third, a kind CEO gives in easily. Giving in in business leads to bankruptcy. We should give in only when there is a valid reason. When we continue to give in without a valid reason, anyone can walk all over us, and there will even be people who brazenly demand that we give in to them.

Fourth, a kind CEO is terrible at chastising others. We must do everything on our own if we hesitate to chastise and give orders to our subordinates, and employees will even point out that this is the undisputed prerogative of the CEO. Worse still, there are employees who will ask their CEO, 'I am working, so why are you doing nothing?'

Fifth, a kind CEO is unduly worried. Worrying further exacerbates a situation. What you have worried about beforehand will unfold in accordance with your worries. Undue worry is neither solace nor reassurance. It often dampens the company's mood and makes everyone around the CEO feel frustrated, or it fills the company with oversensitive people.

Sixth, a kind CEO laughs constantly. No one feels constrained when they laugh all the time. There are many occasions when the CEO requires dignity more than benevolence. Laughter is good, but too much is as bad as too little of it. Excessive laughter becomes poison.

Seventh, it's difficult for a kind CEO to seek help. The things we can accomplish alone in this world are few and far between. The fact that our buttocks are within hands' reach means we can go to the toilet on our own. Everything else should be accomplished with other people. It's impossible to run a business staffed by employees if the CEO struggles to ask for help. In that case they should work in a one-person company. A CEO must make decisions, give orders and check on the business every day. A kind person is therefore unable to ensure the smooth execution of the business. Being kind isn't always a good thing. Being kind is a good thing only when the entire world is kind. However, the world has never been kind all at the same time, so I hope you won't be afraid to shed a little kindness. Only then can we afford to stay kind to the people around us, including our family.

38

The Hardest Thing About People Management

I don't know about having one or two employees, but I can empathise with how difficult people management can be when the number of employees increases. Ten is the number that a CEO finds hardest to manage. When there are ten employees, most employees, regardless of their job titles, will often receive instructions directly from the CEO and bypass the orders of their direct superiors.

Usually, the number of employees that can be managed effectively is four to six. If ten employees are placed in two systems, a CEO theoretically only needs to manage two people. But it's realistically impossible to manage only two people in a small business. This is because the CEO must still be directly involved in many aspects of the company.

It's harder to manage five than three employees, and twice as hard to manage ten as five. This leads to a situation in which a CEO gives employees rest days but the CEO themselves must work not just on weekends but on festive holidays too. At this juncture, numerous CEOs feel ashamed of their work and duties, and lose confidence. It becomes harder as the number of employees grows, and it's a period when they feel most acutely how difficult people management can be. But the fortunate thing is the organisation starts to move on its own once there are twenty employees. From then on, the CEO clearly feels that their work becomes less taxing. This is when the costs of a CEO's direct labour can't match the costs of good management. This is because the company has expanded to a scale where, through good management alone, it's possible to achieve a level of efficiency that surpasses the costs of hiring additional employees.

If the CEO now continues to juggle both practical affairs and business management, the company's growth will go backwards instead. CEOs who hail from a design background should take their hands off the design process, and CEOs who are former chefs should stop cooking. If we intend to sustain a company by our own labour, we will quickly grow weary and hit our limits, or the company will be impeded from expanding further. Once we take our hands off practical affairs, we realise what business management truly means. This is when the organisation and system are both at work.

A company with ten employees and a company with twenty employees are never the same. When there are ten employees, there is no need for order, hierarchy or a special approval system. However, when the number of employees exceeds twenty or thirty, there will be employees who don't know each other's names, and the company must learn to perform tasks through meetings or by obtaining approvals. This is when a CEO oversees only the management of the business and gradually begins to have time on their hands, and there is a reasonable number of backup employees to undertake external projects.

When the number of employees exceeds fifty, the CEO will need a secretary, and everyone will want to sit next to the CEO when they visit the company cafeteria. This is a period when the CEO becomes distant from the employees, because the CEO is supported by employees who wish to replace or stand in for positions that have been vacated after someone has resigned, but it's also a period during which the CEO feels most at ease.

When the number exceeds hundred, the company resembles a mid-sized company, factions are formed, everything is documented, and a structure becomes established in which things are carried out by obtaining approval. Once a company's employees exceed twenty, no matter how much more the number grows, the CEO will feel more at ease than when they were commanding ten employees, because now they can limit the number of employees that receive direct orders to four or five.

But it's no easy feat to grow a ten-person company into one with twenty or thirty employees. Typically, a CEO's management skills fall short, the company is unable to grow beyond ten employees, and progress becomes sluggish. There are also stories where CEOs who haven't learned to effectively manage ten employees ultimately miss out on opportunities to operate businesses that need more than twenty or thirty people. In other words, even CEOs who have around ten employees should learn in advance the lessons they will need when they have more than ten employees if they wish to form such a big company.

The biggest cause of stress for CEOs isn't competitors, markets or customers. Employees give CEOs the biggest stress. The stress of persuading, coaxing, teaching and managing employees is most taxing on CEOs. Therefore, as CEOs grow older, their commonest behaviour is to surround themselves with people who understand and believe in them.

I believe a CEO can take on the entire world if they have five competent employees who believe in them. This is because the five can rule over five thousand.

39

Change the Rules

I had a meeting with a senior executive from a food distribution company. He was conducting separate interviews with ten companies like ours. They were interviews to discontinue partnerships with companies that had fallen short of his company's standards, and to reduce the number of partner companies to just a few. In so doing, he wanted to help the remaining companies grow and improve their product quality and sales methods.

All the company representatives attended the meetings after preparing extensive materials about what their companies excelled in and how much they had grown so far. The meetings were rife with thick prospectuses and every kind of material, including large pamphlets and actual menus. Because their elimination during the meetings would lead to the death of their companies.

We altered our strategy. We focused on what the other company wanted, rather than explaining what we excelled in. We studied the business exhaustively from their perspective. The senior executive intended to discontinue partnerships with some companies, as he planned to raise industry standards and manage the partners simply, and consequently to increase sales. And by highlighting his ability to run the business by increasing sales, he would also have an opportunity to demonstrate to shareholders his stature as a potential candidate for president. We discovered from a report on listed companies that his company's average sales by store size were more than four percent lower than their competitors'. This implied that their sales were higher than their competitors' but efficiency per store had declined. We decided to touch on this point.

Our company noticed that the highest sales had come from small stores. Average sales per square foot across all their stores were only $742. Their competitors were making $771 per square foot on average. On the other hand, our stores in some of their outlets were making average sales of $2,080. Therefore, we calculated for the senior executive the nationwide increase in sales he would gain if he included our stores in every outlet he was managing, and we asked him to pay attention to the point that average sales per square foot could also keep his competitors at bay. He was totally captivated. He knew this was an opportunity for him to cement his position in his company and make his name known to the entire industry.

While other companies were preparing extensive materials, all we put together was a four-page document. Even so, what reached his hands was a single sheet of paper bearing our proposal to increase sales per square foot. After meeting with the senior executive, our competitors were apprehensive, as they were eager to know if they had been selected or eliminated. But we had already altered the senior executive's initial plan and reshaped the market according to our own rules. Our competitors were competing without knowing the rules had changed. As a result, we weren't just one of the fourteen selected by the food distribution company, but the company that represented all fourteen. In less than two years, our company came in first among the fourteen companies, absorbed forty-five percent of the outlets that the senior executive managed, and accounted for sixty percent of total sales.

We didn't try to sell what we wanted. We could sell what we wanted because we decided to sell what *he* wanted. Negotiation and bargaining are ultimately about getting what we want by giving the other party what they want. I am not a beggar.

Some days ago, I sounded out a South Korean conglomerate about doing business with them. They told me I had to produce a proposal of more than forty pages if I wanted to work with them. When I asked why, they said applicants looked serious only if they did so. Furthermore, the people concerned constantly gave me the impression that the South Korean conglomerate would be doing us a favour if our proposal got off the ground. I fully respect their decision to turn us down because they think that working with us won't be helpful to them. But we are unable to work with companies that are structured to yield unilateral gains, or are conscious of doing so. It should be a mutual relationship in which we give them what they want and they give us what we want: a business partnership underpinned by one-sided gains will eventually fall apart. How foolish it is to consider first and foremost how serious we are based on the quality and quantity of our proposal, rather than being interested in how much both parties could benefit from the proposal we submitted.

I instruct the marketing officers in our company not to sell our system if we aren't better than our competitors. I also instruct them not to petition customers to buy our products, but to add value to the products so that customers are compelled to buy them. All bargaining is ultimately about addressing one another's needs equally. It becomes begging if we have little to give, and we are no different from bullies if we take too much.

40

How to Increase Customers Tenfold

We can create ten customers when we satisfy one. But we drive away ten existing customers and a hundred future customers when we disappoint one. We use a rather comprehensive approach in the service business. We need to consider all factors if we wish to satisfy our customers, including pricing, product quality, cleanliness, friendliness and so on. Customers leave when we overlook any of these factors. They may leave even if we fulfil all these factors. This is because of changing times and trends. Moreover, in the cases of ordinary restaurants and hair salons, the percentage of one-time customers who don't return after one visit is much higher than we think. It's closer to seventy percent than to twenty or thirty percent. We can calculate this data accurately by tracking the breakdown of credit card usage.

There are countless occasions during which the marketing expenditure to bring a new customer into a store outweighs the customer's spending. The best way to increase sales is ultimately to draw the one-time customer back again. This is the biggest reason why we should give the warmest welcome to customers who visit our stores. From the perspective of a business owner, we must bear in mind how remarkable it is that every single customer has stepped into our stores, and strive to do our utmost to satisfy each one of them.

Most entrepreneurs inject considerable effort and money into securing new customers. But wise entrepreneurs know it's significantly more effective to focus expenditure or effort on one-time customers. Entrepreneurs make enormous advertising expenditures and offer discounts and limited-time deals at near cost price to lure new customers, but don't push themselves as hard to convert new customers into regular customers. They go out to catch other fish after placing the fish they have caught in a net full of holes.

People are often under the illusion that pricing is the power that draws customers. Pricing is only one of the factors that draws customers; pricing isn't everything. It's actually one of the smallest factors among many others. When you consider your preferred stores or the businesses you frequent, you will easily recognise that you patronise them not just because their products are cheap. When consumers spend money, they spend it on value. The only time identical industrial products compete in the same commercial district is when customers find value in cheap prices. In Jungfraujoch, Switzerland, South Korean instant cup noodles cost $7 per cup. We can buy them at seventy cents per cup in South Korean convenience stores, but there is a different value in gobbling down instant noodles with the Alps at our feet. Therefore, all the South Koreans who visit Jungfraujoch consume instant cup noodles there. Executives who focus on the belief that consumers are concerned solely with pricing have failed.

We must strive to create value in our products and stores for consumers. We must create reasons for them to visit our stores and buy our products. Fortunately, there are many reasons for them to do so. There are countless specific values we can create: good health, a sense of luxury, a sense of stability, a sense of morality, a sense of connectedness, a sense of curiosity, convenience, beauty care, a sense of social responsibility, informativeness, fascination and so on. Therefore, if you aspire to become a competent entrepreneur, you must consider selling value and not products to consumers. We run a business, but we are consumers and customers too. We will find all the answers when we carefully deliberate about how we ourselves wish to be treated, how we purchase products and in what kind of stores. As soon as we focus on selling value and not products to customers, we grow as entrepreneurs rather than traders. This is the most fundamental structure and principle of all businesses.

41

Selecting the Best Talents

When we interview prospective employees, almost every applicant strives to explain the kind of person they currently are. People aren't all born equal. They usually choose a university based on their exam scores, and then they step out into society and lead different lives.

People believe that the hard work they put in to enter a good university was fair competition, and they regard and speak of the universities they attended as symbols of who they are. Consequently, they even make the insolent mistake of asking others at first meeting which universities they graduated from. They presume everyone has been to university, and can't hide the way they rank people according to the universities they attended. Everyone's home environment since birth, and the educational levels of their parents, are different. There are many people who can't afford to attend university, and there are also people who can't take special private lessons or study in a comfortable environment.

It's an unconcealable fact around the world that there is a high probability that those who reside in affluent areas and were born to educated parents will enter university.

A few exceptions can't be used to justify all cases. That said, highly educated individuals and graduates from the best universities demand exceptional treatment because they have come out ahead in this fair game. But we shouldn't evaluate them based on their current merits. We should evaluate them based on how far they have come from where they first began. Life resembles a marathon race in which we all have different starting points. There is no guarantee that someone who sprinted at first, or who had piggybacked on their parents, will run fast all their life.

To me, the best employee is someone who makes progress every month. It doesn't matter if they are slow. An employee who makes a little progress over time is a significantly better employee than a conceited employee whose work ability is outstanding but who behaves as if there is nothing more to learn. The employee who makes progress every month earnestly desires to learn anything they can because they know their inadequacies. Their loyalty and affection for the company are hence strong. Conversely, there are numerous competent employees who thrive initially before coming to a halt at a boundary, as if with bated breath. They have reached their limits. But they attempt to boast or bargain to conceal these limits, and invariably resign when those attempts don't work. Consequently, as executives recognise that it's possible to invest in employees who make monthly progress, they send them for training and business trips, and modify their job titles. But executives can't expect anything from employees who boast about the present, except for their current work.

Moreover, one's employees shouldn't consist only of those who share similar views as the CEO or top students.

I have a poor memory for the names of things and places, and am not especially talented in discerning the characteristics of things. I have a poor memory for numbers too. But I have a special talent. Talent for recognising trees and plants. I can recognise the wild chives and plantains growing by the roadside when I pull the car over on the expressway, and I can identify edible plants. I can tell pretty well what tree it is just by looking at the leaves, because I have a good memory for the subtle distinctions of autumn maple leaves and the unique shapes of fruit trees. Apricot trees, peach trees and cherry trees that bloom in spring may look the same to others, but they are very different trees to me. This might be because my affection for trees and plants is stronger than for numbers and other things.

Perhaps that is why I enjoy planting fruit trees or flowering trees here and there around my house and office whenever I have time. It isn't very exhilarating to stop by the garden and choose as many trees as possible with sturdy stems and upright branches, and then load a heap of them onto a truck. It isn't easy to dig pits, but I am so delighted to see them grow after planting them.

When I return from business trips, I always look at and touch the trees I have planted. However, having planted countless upright trees, I have noticed something odd. Surprisingly, after these trees have grown, they look less graceful than the crooked and unattractive trees I picked up cheaply. Children that resemble stiff, tall trees fill our back garden indistinguishably.

It's strange, but trees that have seemingly grown crooked or fallen look lovely, like gifted models in striking poses, when they stand at year's end. Although the trees won't be used as timber, there are many stiff, tall trees that have grown without expression, looking as dull as if they were posing for a group photo.

The same applies to people. Let's imagine filling an office with only employees who excelled in their studies and were model students. They are employees who work in perfect order and fare well only as instructed. This isn't the military. It's a company where creativity and originality should permeate. The more diverse our academic backgrounds and experiences, the better. And people with different personalities or working styles should work together. Our teams should comprise diverse individuals, including those who clearly possess strong leadership skills, administrators who are competent in administrative work, planners with abundant ideas, and practical workers who enjoy working on simple tasks in silence. And when people of similar academic backgrounds, places of origin, religions or political views are gathered, they will eventually lose their abilities to analyse critically, because their perceptions will grow more alike.

Companies must maintain an open attitude to recognising and maintaining this diversity in order to grow in a balanced way. CEOs should actively encourage the integration of diverse employee types, and retain employees who will aid this integration in companies.

The more my company grows, the more I feel that people are the heart of my business. When I see someone being passionate about their work, wherever they are, I can't simply pass them by. When I see these talented individuals – it doesn't matter if they are parking attendants, hotel employees, flight attendants or company representatives – I will stop walking and wonder whether to ask for their phone numbers. I can't help being greedy when I imagine them making continuous progress every day, every month and every year to come. People come first in business too.

42

How to Make Employees Work Independently

I have personally dubbed my business management style 'Laozi management'. The following verse appears in chapter seventeen of Laozi's *Dao De Jing*:

> The greatest rulers are hardly known by their people.
> The lesser rulers are loved and praised by their people.
> The even lesser rulers are feared by their people.
> The least rulers are despised by their people.
> (太上，下知有之；其次，親而譽之；其次，畏之；其次，侮之)

This is how it looks when adapted for contemporary companies:

The greatest CEOs are hardly known by their employees. Employees therefore fight their own battles. The lesser CEOs are loved and respected by their employees. Employees therefore work with them. The even lesser CEOs are feared by their employees. Employees therefore do whatever they are told, with all their might. The lowest-grade CEOs are scorned by their employees. Employees therefore get to work only when they see their CEO.

Only twenty years ago, I was the lowest-grade CEO. After failing repeatedly, I tried to be a fierce CEO and a friendly CEO. Sometimes I succeeded, sometimes I failed. However, as soon as I passed the age of forty and grew more experienced as a CEO, I decided to observe the teachings of Laozi, a teacher I have always esteemed.

I rise at five o'clock, have a simple breakfast, and go to work before six o'clock. I check emails that arrived in the night and send replies or issue instructions. I look at a few must-visit websites. I look mainly at news and economic indexes, trending jokes, and information on trends and exhibitions. I am mostly done by half past seven.

None of our employees has come to work yet. I leave the office lights on while I look at the state of the documents and things scattered on desks and attempt to guess who has been working hard. After circling the office, I stop by the warehouse, and go around the research development office or the dormitory. If I leave the lights on, I can step out and survey the trees and flowers in the office garden before returning to the office again. By then the employees who come to work early will have started to stream in.

I have simple thirty-minute meetings with the president or vice-president on Mondays, but we don't arrange separate meetings when we are on business trips, and they update me through text messages and emails. There are also barely any company meetings in a year. I don't feel the need to hold additional meetings, because when I have instructions to give or there is a need to clarify something, it suffices to assemble the respective parties separately in KakaoTalk group chats where we can clarify and discuss with one another. Nine o'clock. Our employees are all here and starting to work, but my work has just ended.

In our company the delegation of authority is well enforced, the environment in which employees find their work independently continues like a tradition, and we can maintain remarkable yearly growth even without having anyone who specially issues instructions. I have dozens of truly wonderful employees. Although we open a few new stores every week, they aren't rushed off their feet or confused, and everyone looks composed and experienced. Occasionally, when I run into new employees in the morning, they ask me who I am. There are only a handful of employees who know my personal phone number, and I may receive one or two work-related calls throughout the week, or receive none for several weeks.

Store owners have no idea who I am, so I can comfortably survey whichever store I visit across the country. I leave work at half past ten or, if a little later, I have lunch with employees in the company cafeteria before leaving work. All employees work nine to four, five days a week, and rest on public holidays. I don't come into the office on holidays and weekends either.

You may say that anyone can perform the role of a CEO, but it's possible to operate a company without always being present in the office only if one is willing to forfeit two things. They are interference and a sense of entitlement.

If we point out our employees' mistakes whenever they commit them at work, they will lose heart and not learn from them. Also, if we become overly involved in their projects, they can't make independent judgements and will always depend on their superiors. Sometimes, when there is an obvious blunder that won't ruin the company, I wait and leave it so that employees can subsequently learn from it. We must sometimes hold back even if we are infuriated. If we are unable to hold back and choose to interfere, we may need to dismiss the relevant employees.

If we aspire to construct an office environment where each employee can preserve their creativity, present their views about company rules freely, and find their own work independently, the worst thing that can happen is undue interference. When we are in the passenger seat teaching someone to drive, we can't teach the novice driver by slapping them in the face when they blunder. When the teacher becomes overly agitated or startled at the slightest mistake, the driver will be overwhelmed with fear, unable to think, and will become dependent on others. We can't teach driving in this state, and it could also lead to a major accident. We must possess remarkable courage and audacity if we choose to suppress our screams and not to step on the brakes even when danger is in sight.

Forfeiting the second thing – our sense of entitlement – is possible only when we defeat an entrepreneur's primitive instincts. Money and honour are sometimes people's motivations for doing business and aspiring to succeed. This honour may include our intention to avenge ourselves for the humiliation we suffered as a child, as well as to prove ourselves to those who have believed in us. There are also people who simply want others to look up to them while they look down on those under them. There is a fundamental materialistic quality to success in business. There is power when money grows. It offers not political power, but the power to completely transform someone's life when we set our minds to it.

Humans long for, fear and are in awe of this power. It's humans' most primitive instinct to desire to have one more person recognise that one has such authority and power. I am now asking you to relinquish that desire.

Do not insist on occupying the top seat in the office; queue with your food tray, wait your turn and have your meal; do not be disappointed because external visitors didn't ask to meet you; do not wait for the car door to be opened for you. Instead, hold the door for female employees when they are walking behind you, do not tactlessly linger at company dinners, do not be disappointed when no one asks you to officiate at their wedding, and above all, do not rashly condescend to employees, asking them to pick up the tab.

You shouldn't attempt to be the king, but to be the crown of the company. You can retain authority, dignity, the essence of the business and your role as the company's symbol, but let your subordinates do the work and represent the company.

There is freedom even in doing business when interference and a sense of entitlement cease. There is no need to be dragged to this and that inconsequential gathering, and there are no unneeded expenditures that will cause heartache. No one will bad-mouth me even if I wander around in farmer's overalls, as no one recognises me; and most of all, I can spend a good deal of time with my family. Even so, our company continues to run as a company should. The subjects know they have a king, but they don't know who the king is, and they aren't afraid. For that reason, it's a peaceful reign. The only problem is my wife grouses that I leave work too early. That is inevitable. I can't permit a situation in which my wife has a husband but doesn't know who he is.

Part 4

The Miracle of Repeating Your Goals a Hundred Times a Day for a Hundred Days

There is a simple way to know if our goals are truly what we desire above anything else. If you are bent on achieving them, do not be content with writing them on paper, and repeat them a hundred times daily for a hundred days. They are indeed your truly desired goals if you do this for a hundred days. This is because you won't see the point of doing it and will stop midway if they aren't your truly desired goals. Writing or repeating our goals a hundred times daily for a hundred days isn't as easy as we think. When I try to do this, I sometimes don't recall whether I have done it, and I ask myself why I should do it. I have written such goals on paper a hundred times to realise them. Of all the goals that have gone through this exercise, there isn't one that I haven't achieved.

43

The Problem with Immoderate Kindness

I had visited the local Department of Public Safety to renew my driving licence. Since early morning, countless people had been queuing out of the door to take their driving tests. After a civil servant conducted a simple eye test and finished asking questions about donating my organs and exercising my voting rights in case of an accident, he sent me back to sit and wait. But there was no vacant wall I could lean against, let alone vacant seats, so I mostly stared awkwardly at the ceiling.

The incident occurred after I found a seat and was about to flip open the newspaper in my hands to read it. A woman in her thirties who was sitting beside me hesitated before walking five or six steps diagonally. She then grabbed a gentleman's elbow and said, 'Grandpa, have a seat here.' If I hadn't closely observed the gentleman's expression at that moment, and if I weren't describing this situation in detail and had ended the story here, it would have simply slipped by as an ordinary act of kindness by a young newlywed who offered her seat to an elderly man and made me ashamed of not having stood up earlier.

The gentleman whom the young woman had called 'grandpa' looked older than sixty but appeared virile nevertheless, and apart from his proliferating white hair it was absurd to call him 'grandpa'. He wasn't slouching, he did not look frail, and he wasn't looking about for a vacant seat. However, for the first time in his life, he heard a young woman call him 'grandpa' and suffered the indignity of being offered a seat.

I felt too embarrassed to watch on as the gentleman's facial expressions instantly transformed to show perplexity, embarrassment and the sense of defeat that was rising within him. Now what had this woman done? The woman's thoughtless kindness had announced, in the presence of many people, 'You are no longer a man'.

Small acts of kindness can save lives and gladden people forever. But immoderate kindness can be perilous. When I drive out of my house and attempt to enter a four-lane road, sometimes there are kind drivers who stop their cars and tell me to pass through first, even though they have right of way. But I could have a major accident with a vehicle whizzing past in the next lane if I were to trust their giving way to me and head right out.

The immoderate kindness of entrepreneurs too can distress employees and the company, and stifle growth. CEOs perceive employees as targets to be taught, or as subordinates who can always be condescended to and who are relatively ignorant in all respects. They therefore speak to them thoughtlessly, as though speaking to their youngest siblings, and they are under the illusion that they are doing so out of affection for their subordinates and consider themselves superb superiors. To be precise, employees are only subordinates at work, not subordinates in life. They are individuals who could have been brilliant friends and teachers, despite their young age and low rank, if we had met them outside work. But CEOs interfere in more than just work and speak thoughtlessly to employees solely because they are their subordinates at work. This implies that there would be no reason for a CEO to be admonished with 'This isn't the way to live' because of their own incompetence or poor performance.

Sometimes there are instances when businesses suffer due to immoderate kindness towards consumers or markets. Immoderate kindness towards South Korean product names seeking to penetrate overseas markets is a classic problem. I wish South Korean *gotgam* were labelled *gotgam*. Not dried persimmons. *Bindaeddeok* is *bindaeddeok*; why is it called Korean pizza? Why is *ddeok* called rice cake, confusing consumers and markets? It isn't Korean popcorn but *gangnaengi*. This form of kindness can't create new markets. Consumers suffer too, as they can't recognise the differences. In business the one who adopts a new phraseology first wins, but kind entrepreneurs seem to think that foreigners don't have the mental capacity to embrace new words.

Additionally, CEOs who give excessive instructions about the minutest details shouldn't expect employees to exercise their creativity. When they interpret details in this manner, designers or chefs become technicians, vice-presidents become spokespersons, and managers become people who don't manage but only await instructions. Kindness resembles a sharpened knife: it can be used to prepare delectable food if used well, but it can also be used to inflict pain if used recklessly. The beauty of business is to discover how kind one should be.

The gentleman who was embarrassed when a young woman offered her seat said confidently before the crowd, 'Young lady! Thank you for offering your seat, but I don't think I am at the age to be offered a seat, as I still see you as a woman. So just remain seated.' Some people chuckled.

44

Work Till You No Longer Work for Money

Our company has zero debt. All goods are paid for as soon as we receive them; the accounts for our corporate card are settled fortnightly, as we can't wait a month to do that; our office building was paid for in cash. We have never taken out loans to purchase office supplies, including our dozens of cars.

As a company, we don't pay a single cent of bank interest. All the companies I own have zero debt. My personal life is no different. I have had no loans for anything I personally own, including houses, cars, properties and so on. My wife and I don't own a single personal credit card. Even if I go bankrupt tomorrow, electricity and water bills will be the only items I must pay off. I don't have any personal or corporate tax arrears or owe outstanding personal debts to anyone.

If you have failed seven times, you will realise how terrifying it is to run into debt. But I now earn far more than I spend every month. I am a major shareholder in an asset management company, and the largest shareholder in a listed company in South Korea. I am now someone who earns as much as the combined annual salaries of several individuals, just from dividends alone. I have become a wealthy man. I have achieved what is often called social success. As our company grows at the high rate of fifty percent yearly, we start another new company like our current one after one or two years. I don't spend much money, as I am not an extravagant person to begin with.

As Walt Disney put it, I have worked to 'a point where you don't work for money'. There is nothing I can't afford at department stores or anywhere I go.

I visited a shopping mall with my wife, and luxury cars were on display. They were gorgeous sports cars. My wife said, 'I can afford them, but I shan't buy them.' Instead of buying them, it was more exhilarating not to buy them, even though we could have afforded to do so right away.

There was nothing we couldn't afford in that enormous department store, but the two of us just had a lunch that cost $16 and then went home. The reason was that not buying anything even though we could afford everything was the same as having everything.

I am in a position where there is nothing more I desire. To get to this day, I have written new goals in my notebook every year. And I have realised these goals by thinking and repeating them endlessly. Then I have erased the realised goals and written new ones.

I have done this for more than twenty years, and so far I have always succeeded in achieving them. Usually I have around twenty goals or dreams every year, but this year I erased them and decided to set five new ones. Because of that, several of the goals set last year vanished before they could be realised. The reason is that the number of things I desire has now decreased considerably, because over more than thirty years I have achieved everything I longed to have or do. However, although the number of goals has decreased, their size has grown. I may have been motivated by the fact that two of my friends have entered the 'Forbes 400' list of the richest Americans. I couldn't find new reasons to be wealthy, but I simply became curious. I wondered how people at the top of the world lived. I also wondered what kind of friends they would meet. And I didn't know if I would be able to use Forbes's reputation to introduce myself to people I have always wanted to befriend. Thus, I wrote down the goal of having my name included on Forbes's list of the wealthiest four hundred Americans. This was the fourth of five newly made goals.

To realise the fourth goal, the very first goal I wrote was to produce a hundred millionaires among my employees, family and community. This was because I supposed I would have to become a billionaire to produce a hundred millionaires in my community. My employees and those around me who discovered I had this goal were exhilarated. They were quite curious to know if they were included on the list of hundred people. With this goal in mind, I altered our company's annual sales target to $1 billion. This was the second goal. This target changed to $1 billion before we had even achieved the target of $500 million, which had been conceived two years before. The third and fifth are very personal goals.

This was how I organised the five goals. As I had realised almost every goal noted down so far and believed that I could achieve these new goals, I often envisioned scenarios in which these new goals had indeed been realised, and I examined myself to see if there were any problems with realising them. There is a simple way to know if our goals are truly what we desire above anything else. If you are bent on achieving them, do not be content with writing them on paper, and repeat them a hundred times daily for a hundred days. They are indeed your truly desired goals if you do this for a hundred days. This is because you won't see the point of doing it and will stop midway if they aren't your truly desired goals. Writing or repeating our goals a hundred times daily for a hundred days isn't as easy as we think. When I try to do this, I sometimes don't recall whether I have done it, and I ask myself why I should do it.

I have written such goals on paper a hundred times to realise them. Of all the goals that have gone through this exercise, there isn't one that I haven't achieved. As the goals this time relate specifically to business targets, four subordinates and I have been writing out the goals a hundred times daily and taking pictures of them before uploading them to our common chat room. We upload the pictures even during holidays and overseas business trips. We have just passed the ninety-first day at the time of writing this book. None of us has withdrawn from this exercise. We will have passed the hundredth day before this book is published. We will reach our goals more easily because we are doing it together.

I still ask myself whether I would be slightly happier if I were wealthier than I am now. I often hear that the life of a wealthy person isn't a very happy one. We are sometimes comforted by the misadventures of lottery winners who struck gold. Is that true? I have lived in destitution and affluence. I worked three years without resting a single day, I was so destitute I couldn't afford instant noodles, and for several years I dreaded getting calls from the bank every morning and my hair fell out because my businesses were at risk of bankruptcy.

Conversely, now there is always money left in my pockets no matter how much I spend, I can purchase as many books as I want from bookshops without looking at the price tags, I can gift houses to my parents and parents-in-law or send them on trips at every change of season, I buy luxury cars without using credit, and purchase houses worth millions of dollars using the money I have earned in three months. Even so, the same amount of money comes in the next month. No doubt I haven't lived in abject poverty, and my company hasn't grown into a colossal conglomerate, but having experienced both ends of the spectrum, I think it's still far more desirable to live as a wealthy man.

Many of our worries are associated with money. If you write out ten of your present worries, and write the remedies next to each worry, you will be surprised how many worries can be remedied with money. Money clearly makes humans more comfortable and respectable. I wish to grant this freedom to at least a hundred people around me. I know full well that my desire to be included on *Forbes*'s list of the wealthiest four hundred Americans, just to satisfy my own curiosity, sounds boastful and frivolous in this competitive modern society. Nonetheless, I wish to climb the ladder, like a child who wonders what's on the roof. I fear I might break my legs.

However, if I set myself up as a manager rather than an owner of wealth, I know that whenever I wish to come down again, there will be a hundred people waiting for me, holding the ladder so that I can come down.

45

Gathering Powerful People Around the World

I have developed a bold habit as I have grown older: immediately asking to be friends whenever I meet good people. There are currently pastors and company representatives among those I have met under such circumstances. I have done this for more than a decade. I once wrote a series of columns for a newspaper. There were readers who read the columns and exchanged emails with me. We met several times when I visited South Korea, and the more we met, the more I grew fond of them. When I met up with my classmates when we were younger, we couldn't really connect, perhaps because, apart from our shared memories, the trajectories of our lives were different. I felt as if we had hiked a mountain together but were now looking at each other from opposite mountaintops. Conversely, I felt as if I were scaling the same mountain with friends I had met belatedly midway.

This was how I met Jin-Goo Yoo. He was a few years older than me, but I wanted to be his friend rather than his younger brother. I sought his understanding, and we became candid friends. I discovered later that he was two years my senior at university, but it was already too late. We don't stand on ceremony with each other, and we aren't concerned or disappointed when we don't hear from each other. We are as delighted as ever when we do hear from each other, and out of the blue we send each other inane text messages, and remain on good terms even if we simply read them without replying. Now, because of this providential friendship, we are operating a business together, our families mingle, and our friendship continues. I don't deserve a friend like him. This is because although I call him my friend, he is like a teacher to me.

Among all the people I have personally met, I have never seen anyone wiser than Jin-Goo. He is a person who has a gift for hearing people out, who knows the art of respecting people irrespective of rank, who isn't partial to certain ideas or teachings, and who knows how to think independently. You have no idea how valuable my life has become because a friend like him appeared. How fortunate I was not to have met just anybody when I felt alone.

One day, I learned by chance that a neighbourhood pastor who had visited our company had been born in the same year and at the same time as me. Intrigued, we chatted and became friends. Our condition for becoming friends was simple. We agreed to respect one another. The condition was: he wouldn't invite me to church, and in return I would welcome him as an ordinary person rather than a clergyman. We sometimes exchange text messages, and it's invariably amusing when we do so using informal speech. It's also delightful to send each other greetings on our birthday.

Who said it's hard to make friends as we grow older? Getting into new romantic relationships at this age might be scandalous, but new friendships invariably make our lives worthwhile. A senior of mine who will soon be retiring made a novel remark. He said we needed many friends when we grew older, so I asked him why, and he said, 'They keep dying.'

Once, when I visited a company in Los Angeles, I met an executive whose personality I liked instantly. Humans can read one another, so I shook his hand and asked to be friends. The look on this man's face when he received this request – on the spot, from a man he had met at work and who was well over fifty – was hilarious. But this man had probably read *The Romance*

of the Three Kingdoms[15] several times, as I had. I asked for his friendship and said clearly that I wanted to be friends with him. It's evidently embarrassing behaviour. However, we shouldn't just ask people we like of the opposite gender for their number. We can also ask an excellent prospective friend for their number.

The friend I met in this way is Seong-Won Ra. This friend has a remarkable ability to instantly code-switch between languages, and takes extraordinary pride in his work and the industry. Although he is a wonderfully religious man, he doesn't make others feel uncomfortable because of his beliefs. My wife and sister-in-law are major fans of his, perhaps because he knows what women want to hear and understands women's feelings. Above all, he is cheerful and loyal. I have been invited to his home, treated to sumptuous food, and introduced to his children, so I know what they are like. We have a great deal to catch up on because we met when we were older. Although I can't see him often, as he frequently travels for business, he sends me text messages from around the world. When we happen to be in the same country and the same city, we will replace our pining with an impromptu meeting.

There have also been occasions when my wife and I became friends with other couples. Once, I was sipping tea in a departure lounge when a woman strode straight towards me from the opposite side of the room. Sometimes I meet people I know on a plane, but I couldn't recall who she was. I recalled her only after she said hello, called out my wife's name and said, 'You're Mi-Yeong's husband, aren't you?' She was the mother of a bright and popular child who attended the same school as my eldest. We had met a few times at

---

15 Translator's note: *The Romance of the Three Kingdoms* is a Chinese historical novel set at the end of the Han dynasty and during the Three Kingdoms period of Chinese history. It dramatises and romanticises how the three kingdoms vied to rule China after the collapse of the Han dynasty.

school when our children were younger, but we hadn't introduced ourselves. She and her husband were a wonderful couple. But that was a time when I hadn't yet acquired the boldness to ask to be friends with strangers, and feeling demoralised by the impressiveness of this already successful couple, I hadn't dared to ask to be friends with them.

As soon as Paul's mother met someone in a foreign airport who lived in the same neighbourhood as she did, she hid her feelings of unfamiliarity with great joy, and requested an introduction. After this providential encounter, we went home and had dinner together with our spouses. The women sympathised with each other and were amused by their similarities as wives whose husbands ran businesses, and the men shared the regrets they had felt when they both embarked on the same route to establish themselves in a new society they had migrated to. Like people in love, we two couples were attracted to each other and met frequently. Since we live a five-minute drive away from each other, we don't stand on ceremony with each other, we exercise together, drink tea late at night, and hang out without watching the clock. If Paul's mother, Hyeon-Joo Lee, hadn't approached me then, we wouldn't have had this providential friendship, and I wouldn't have had met Hong-Beom, a wonderful gentleman.

There is no need to worry about age when making new friends. I have now mustered the courage to ask to be friends whenever I meet good people. When you consider powerful people around the world, they ask to form friendships with one another irrespective of age, gender or social status. If I hadn't had this boldness, I wouldn't have acquired these friends. When I think of living without them, I wonder how I would fill the emptiness inside me. I would be exasperated, pondering how I should live the rest of my days. My childhood classmates don't offer practical value to my life now, just as former lovers no longer offer value to my life now. Therefore, I hope to step out into the world, convert acquaintances into close friends around me, and enjoy the rest of my life.

Be a father and friend to your children.
If it seems you must choose one of the two,
choose to be a father.
Because they will have many friends, even without you,
but they only have one father – you.

Draw closer when you pee.
It isn't just tears that
men shouldn't shed.

Do not expect filial piety when raising your children. I too received
it in full while raising you, from the way you smiled and grew up.

Extract from 'Twenty-Six Lessons for My Sons' in
Note on Self-Management

46

Self-Determination

I have self-determination if I have done what I desired to do and can live the same way in the future. But I don't have self-determination if I have been doing what I don't desire to do and will likely continue to do so in the future.

Life without self-determination is no different from slavery. It's the most rightful and blessed thing in the lives of humans to live in an environment where we can work independently, in a career we like and have chosen. There will be people who say, 'There is nothing I can decide for myself right now.' However, if we pause and reflect, we see that we are where we are right now as a result of the countless decisions that we have made so far. We always have opportunities to change our environment. I have no idea at what midway point some of us have conceded defeat. And even if we have conceded defeat, that could have been our decision.

The happiness of human beings is determined by the number of decisions we can make independently. The reason we make money is also to ensure our self-determination. Much of our right to rest when we wish, do what we want, and refuse to do what we don't want has to do with money. Almost everything has to do with money. No doubt there are numerous instances in which we can't obtain what we want with money, but the previous sentence isn't an incorrect statement when we consider how much financial independence controls our lives. But there are many examples of wealthy people who are also unable to properly exercise self-determination. This is because they consider money to be a goal rather than a means to an end.

After all, self-determination begins with freedom of thought rather than quantities of assets. People who have freedom of thought have perfect self-determination when they have money. Freedom of thought begins with not relinquishing the right to think independently. You must reflect independently as to whether your current thoughts are indeed your own thoughts. Our thoughts contain other thoughts that cause us to think that our thoughts are our own.

Remorse, popular opinion, lack of historical awareness, desperation, statistics, long-standing dreams, gullibility, greed, religion, ill health and so on stop us from thinking independently.

A leader is generally someone who can think and judge independently in any situation. I delight in taking solitary walks around the neighbourhood in the morning or evening, without listening to a phone or music. When I reflect as I walk, I experience flashes of illumination, just like when I am hit on my calves, and I see myself searching for my true mind and thoughts.

I hope you will reread and reflect on your religious scriptures independently, no matter what your religious leaders have said. God hasn't given them a special ability to interpret scriptures just because they are religious leaders. I hope you will consider the disparities between past and present before you decide to follow what your seniors told you were the right methods. This is because there are countless instances when wholly contradictory methods can be used strategically in tandem with the changing times. Do not believe that you can emulate the stories in good self-help books after reading them in bookshops. A huge number of self-help books aren't about the authors' own experiences and are textbooks written by people who just call themselves experts.

Although sometimes the authors describe first-hand experiences, most stories have been embellished and exaggerated during the writing process, after the authors have already succeeded, so it's perilous to emulate them as they are written. It's like an automated stock-trading program: equations formed on the basis of past results can't guarantee tomorrow's winning rate. It's the same reason why it might be a sham when a clever fortune teller who has ascertained our past attempts to tell our future.

I hope you will always think independently and then exercise self-determination aright.

When a plane crash occurs, everyone feels a sense of horror and decides to travel by car instead. Although travelling by plane is considerably safer than by car, the latter is preferred, because we aren't the ones steering the plane, and so we think there would be nothing we could do if we were caught in a precarious situation.

There are people who feel carsick when they get into the back of a car, or who feel all right when they are tickled but will die if someone's hand comes near their belly. These are all manifestations of fear, because these people have no self-determination. Self-determination builds us up and helps us overcome fear.

When we learn and continue to think independently and exercise self-determination, a wonderful life that is uniquely ours is conceived.

47

Trade or Business

If I had planned to make money by selling bento boxes during the early days of my current business, and if I had succeeded, by now I would have become the owner of three or four restaurants. But I started a franchise business without even knowing what a franchise business was. It was a franchise business because I wanted to sell a system, not food. The reason was that I wasn't a chef, and I was interminably greedy.

I have always wished to operate a business and not to trade. Each time I founded a company, I would concede defeat along the road that runs from trading to operating a business. There will be people who question the difference between trade and business. There are two major differences. One is the perception of markets. A trade focuses only on its neighbourhood. The end goal is to survive in the street. If all goes well, a trader aims to start another store, or to sell their products at premium prices. A business focuses not on the street, but on all its stores. A business increases the number of its directly managed stores, one at a time, when it's confident of managing them and has adequate capital, and when it doesn't have adequate capital or time it opens hundreds of franchises. In other words, a trade is about selling products, and a business is about selling stores.

The second difference lies in a CEO's scope of work when operating a business. Trade is when a CEO does everything better than the employees. Trade is when a CEO is better than the employees at customer service, menu development, staffing cash registers, accounting, advertising, and even putting advertisements on the door, or packaging the food that customers have ordered. Conversely, a competent entrepreneur trains people to perform these tasks better than he or she can. An entrepreneur hires managers who excel in customer service, or trains employees with good character, and encourages and recognises them so that they perform better than the entrepreneur. The entrepreneur also acquires the ability to defend the work of head chefs so that they can produce creative menus, or to make them feel apologetic for not having done their best when stores are suddenly swarmed with customers instead of calling on the CEO to help. The entrepreneur also makes it a point to train part-timers to use cash registers.

You are an entrepreneur when you know how to organise work so that every employee can independently become an expert in an area of work, and you don't need to be knowledgeable about their work. To become such entrepreneurs, we must firmly forbear while our employees grow through their mistakes. Employees are unable to make further progress when we nag or impose punishments on them because of our impatience or evident losses. The moment we impose punishments on them, our employees reach their growth limits, and the CEO will need to do everything else. CEOs with omnifarious talents can operate their businesses effectively at the start, but their businesses can't grow further if they don't transform employees into individuals who can perform each task better than they can. And these CEOs will need to eke out a living by their own labour all their lives.

Whether we survive as a trader or grow as an entrepreneur doesn't depend on how much capital we have. It depends on the magnitude of our minds when we consider the work we do.

One day, I attended an exhibition in Busan, and visited a middle-aged couple I had heard about who operated seafood restaurants. They were operating a few restaurants and faring well. But not long before, a new competitor had suddenly started more than a dozen restaurants in downtown

Busan. The couple found it incomprehensible. They were curious and solicited opinions about why restaurants with standards lower than theirs could so quickly match the achievements they had accumulated over decades.

I replied firmly, 'Because your food is good.' They were flustered. They couldn't understand why providing good food was a problem.

'You would have wished to be chefs rather than entrepreneurs, because you are people who emphasise taste. You would therefore have worked tremendously hard, going around every store and upholding standards of taste. Because of your conscientiousness, with luck you might have owned at least a few stores. But you wouldn't have been able to expand further, because you have only one body each. On the other hand, those young friends, rather than emphasising taste, have focused in their stores on maintaining ordinary standards of taste that aren't disappointing. They have had no problem opening dozens of stores, because they have developed a structured method of managing menus. While you were focused on taste in your trade, the other party became entrepreneurs who focused not on taste but on store ambience, operating structure, business image, market research and so on. Just as good music doesn't receive popular acclaim, delectable food isn't liked by everyone. Taste is subjective, because it depends on the environment.' Only then did the couple smack their knees and return home.

An outstanding trader will operate a renowned restaurant if they truly succeed. However, they can become an entrepreneur operating a mid-sized company that commands hundreds of stores if they learn the method of operating a structured business based on a system. There is a way to take it to the next level from there. Above the entrepreneur, there is the industrialist.

A trader succeeds by focusing on a single business, and an entrepreneur by focusing on a business type, but an industrialist expands by focusing on an entire industry. For instance, if we describe a trader as someone who owns a *ddeokbokki* store, an entrepreneur will be an owner of a chain of *ddeokbokki* stores, and an industrialist will be categorised as someone who leads a flour-based business.

Let's imagine an orchard. There are numerous fruit trees in the orchard. Let each of these trees represent an industry. One of them is a food industry tree. There are huge branches on the tree, divided into the manufacturing business, distribution business, restaurant business and so on, and on the restaurant business branch are smaller branches that are subdivided into Korean food, Japanese food, Chinese food, Italian food, flour-based food and so on. A small branch called Korean food is subdivided again into full-course food, home-cooked food, speciality food, traditional indigenous food and so on, and at the end each leaf forms a field of its own, such as *galgooksoo* and *bibimbap*.

If you are operating a business, you must now decide where you wish to go. The very fortunate thing is that where you set your sights on depends not on how much capital you have, but how big your mind is. If you are satisfied with tree leaves, you should stop reading this chapter. However, if you wish to grab hold of the branches – and if you have the desire to catch hold of thicker branches, and are determined not to flutter in the wind or fall from the tree, even when the seasons change – you should dream of becoming an entrepreneur and not a trader. Surpass this and dream of becoming an industrialist.

If there are no branches to grab hold of, create new branches, or wait where the buds will sprout. The instant you have a branch, not a leaf, in your hands, whatever branch it is, you will be in a position where you aren't fearful of a recession or fad, just as you are undaunted by the wind and seasons.

48

The Economics of Footing the Bill

Between the one who often foots the bill, and the one who backs off whenever it's time to do so – who will become more successful?

My third brother-in-law can't bear to see others foot the bill. He is the type who will pay the bill ten times for ten meals. It must be true when my wife's elder sister says that no one who has visited their home in Masan, South Korea, hasn't had a free meal on them. As he frequently foots the bill because he feels embarrassed to sponge off others, his friends come to accept his gesture, and from then on they never consider paying, and even order exorbitant food to excess. That is the only time he gets cross. My sister-in-law burns with anger because he still pays the bill again next time too.

Conversely, there are also people who never foot the bill or who, as soon as they are seated at the table, look for someone who will pay and then without hesitation thank them for the meal. But the odd thing is that those who often pay the bill know that they do so, but those who don't have no idea that they have been marked as people who never pay. There are quite diverse reasons. The selective-memory types who remember only the times they have paid, the family type who shares food brought from home and counts that as something they have paid for, as well as the entertainer type who performs tricks at the table as a substitute for payment – they all think that they have fulfilled their obligations in their own ways. Moreover, they think that they are merely being frugal, not miserly.

Those who propose beef for a meal when they aren't even paying, those who think that it's right for the other party to pay because they earn more, and those who expect to sponge off others because they themselves are of a lower rank, are all simply misers who depend on the magnanimity of others. People who don't foot the bill will eventually lose all their married friends, their seniors won't stand behind them, and their juniors will ignore them.

They can never succeed, because their tendency to save money and not pay the bill stems from miserliness. No one wants to befriend a miser. Their siblings and parents, and of course their spouses too, will reject them in due course. In the end, not footing the bill is an economic loss. If we dismiss this, we will be totally barred from promotions, business opportunities, inheritances and the benefits of good will.

No matter how financially destitute we are, we must never consider it a free lunch when others foot the bill.

I advise you to at least observe this rule. We should foot the bill once when an elder or a wealthy friend does it twice. However, when a co-worker foots the bill once, we should do it once too. This is a very simple rule.

Even my third brother-in-law, who often foots the bill, has a good memory for people who don't. Even a magnanimous person like him doesn't take care of a miserly friend, aside from paying for their food. People assess one another based on actions smaller than we think. There is no way for all your other virtues to compensate for the fact that you disguise the generosity of others as your own frugality.

To pay is to earn.

49

Praise for Indolence

I want to cook some instant noodles. I pour water into a saucepan and place it on the stove. The water begins to boil (five minutes). I look for a packet of instant noodles, open it, and put the noodles in the saucepan (four minutes). I transfer the fully cooked noodles to a bowl and set the table. I bring out the *kimchi* and search for a pair of chopsticks. I pour a cup of water and bring it to the table (three minutes). It's taken me twelve minutes in total, bustling around diligently.

I adopt a different method this time. As soon as I pour water into the saucepan, I place the noodles straight in. The noodles and cold water begin to cook and simmer together. Meanwhile, I prepare the *kimchi*, a pair of chopsticks and a cup of water. When the noodles are cooked, I place the saucepan on the table (seven minutes). When diligent and indolent methods are applied simultaneously, the noodles are fully cooked in the time it takes just for the water to boil. You may ask what the fuss is about with eating instant noodles more quickly in seven minutes, but when we utilise the efficiency that comes from indolence, the effect resembles getting to live two lives in one lifetime. This is because we can be as indolent as we wish in the time that we save by utilising this efficiency.

I like going to work early in the morning, before our employees do. This is because when I leave for work at around half past five, the roads are clear, and not only can I get to work, but I am not interrupted by anyone and can work peacefully. First, I check my emails. I check all the emails that arrived the day before, and I send emails about the details I need to know and about my instructions. This takes less than fifteen minutes. I look up must-read news and information, and scan for updated information on the websites that I frequent. This takes around an hour.

The sun isn't up yet, but it's rather bright outside. I look around inside the company building. Then I step out and survey the trees and flowers in the company garden to see if they have changed. I have completed my work before nine in the morning. My motivation for spending one or two hours a day operating and managing an organisation that has made hundreds of millions of dollars in sales and employs thousands of employees stems from my desire to be indolent.

Working for long hours doesn't mean a person is coping well, because humans have a limited ability to concentrate. It goes without saying that everyone concentrates on things they are interested in, and when we accept the fact that work is inevitable because it concerns our livelihoods, we can easily recognise that employees have difficulty working long hours.

When we increase our efficiency, eight hours of work can be completed in two hours. Conversely, when the working hours are long, we are bound to add more work to fit the long working hours. Our company starts work at nine in the morning and ends at four in the afternoon. We work for five days a week and rest on all public holidays. When the weather is really bad, we see to it that everyone leaves work early. From the standpoint of each employee, the company isn't the purpose of their lives. It's merely a tool of their lives. This also applies to me, the company owner. It's problematic to expect employees to cherish the company as their own and to work night and day as if working for themselves.

I wish to lay the foundation for all employees so they can be wisely indolent. I wish to construct an indolent environment in which employees can leave work at four after working for several hours, without being conscious of what others think, return to their families, rest throughout the holidays, travel and meet their friends. Would anyone not love such a company?

Over the past eight years, our company has thankfully continued to achieve a high growth rate of eighty percent on average every year. Our company grows twice in size almost every year. We are diligent for the sake of indolence. Indolence is the purpose of diligence.

50

Finding Order in Chaos

People who have achieved remarkable success on the financial market once will invariably think that they have found a special pattern in how the market works, and they will boast about it. Those who trust these people invest as they do, or give them their hard-earned money and ask to share their good fortune, but again and again this good fortune doesn't come to pass. Historically, there have been countless cases of such good fortune. And so far, no one has discovered an order in the future from the past. This order is like water that has escaped from a stream, converging in a river and briefly flowing with the tide before parting. It's a misconception of successful people to presume they can comprehend the flow of the entire stream because of that brief encounter. Those who demonstrate a remarkable talent for finance, social phenomena, trends, future predictions and so on deny that their talent is simply good fortune. In that case, have I succeeded as an entrepreneur by good fortune? Yes, by good fortune.

I learned of the American bento box business when it was coming of age, I could penetrate the market without competitors because I lived in Houston, I was desperately searching for a new business trajectory, and I made it to where I am today because the repeated good fortune I experienced while expanding this market included ideas I had had while I was penniless. Moreover, I learned about distribution. Even now, I am one of the people who knows best about how, in what way and through what structures a product should be displayed in a store, and how many products will be sold. Of those who have this talent, how many Asians have lived in Houston and in my generation? Good fortune is hence clearly at work.

But many successful people don't wish to say that they have succeeded by good fortune. That would make them look a little worthless, and they feel that their hard work somehow won't be recognised. They therefore speak like people who have learned to find order in chaos. And they claim that others can also succeed by applying the rules they have discovered. When they reiterate this claim, they also believe that they themselves have indeed succeeded by these rules. Thus, they organise lectures or impart these rules to their juniors, and devise certain reasonings and formulas. However, if you look inside successful people and ask yourself if they could achieve such success all over again given their experiences, formulas and rules, you will shake your head. Of course, those who have succeeded once have a high possibility of succeeding again. But it's never because they have discovered a pattern or formula for success. Many entrepreneurs end up failing at their second business. The probability is higher for people who are highly conceited about their own successes.

No one in this world has discovered the formula for success. No one has discovered order in chaos. It's possible to partially forecast natural phenomena such as the weather or the trajectory of stars, and to discover a fixed order within them. But things like success and finance are phenomena of human behaviour. We can't find order in this world in any way. Surely we could possess all the money in the world if we had discovered order in the financial world for just half a day, and if we had discovered the formula for success, the secret would circulate instantly, and the world would be filled with only successful people.

Mathematically, we know that a world in which everyone becomes wealthy and successful will never come to pass. This is because wealth and success are relative, which means one is poor if the other is wealthy, and if someone succeeds, there are many others who aren't in that position.

Many people sell the fantasy of order. They are confident that such-and-such a fund will yield the most profits this year because it did the year before, and they boldly announce in the press that interest rates will decrease at year's end, or say confidently that the real-estate market will recover from the third quarter next year – things that even God can't know. These are imprudent remarks. They should be cautious of making such judgements, no matter how remarkable their reputations and titles are. If they truly believed what they said, they would have betted everything they had and instantly become wealthy people, but I haven't yet seen anyone do that. The reason is they know full well how many people have disappeared after trying that.

This is the truth: there is no order in the world of money and success. There is no pattern. There is no eternal victor. The most typical way to survive after succeeding once is to exercise restraint, be cautious, and stay vigilant to guard your success until the day you die. There are far more people who have disappeared after believing that they have discovered a pattern and order than there are successful people. As God runs the world by confusion and chaos, these people have all disappeared after remarking on the world's order, before they could become gods of this world. This is why we should stay humble after we have made our mark, and not treat our juniors with condescension.

51

Give to Receive

We must give something to receive something from others.

We must give our commitment if we want to win a woman's heart. We must give our loyalty if we want to gain the friendship of a friend. We must demonstrate our talents if we want to gain popularity in this world, and we must demonstrate our credibility if we want to make our mark in business.

If there is something we want to have, we must offer something that will substitute the value of that thing. We must forfeit our time and sleep if we want to study, and we must offer our shins if we want to learn roller skating. We must put up with criticisms if we want to become a leader, and we must relinquish our privacy if we wish to become famous. We may also need to give up on our family and a long lifespan if we want to become a CEO.

Nothing is free in this world. To pay nothing is simply to pay a hidden price for seizing the costliest thing. Therefore, if there is something we wish to have, the first thing we should do is decide what we should relinquish. We will never receive what we want if we don't relinquish anything, and the things we receive that seem to cost nothing will demand a severe price, like the interest on a private loan. If you want to succeed, you must be conscientious from the outset, have credibility, work hard and be willing to learn. Everything we have received without doing these things is due to be given back. The easy road is crowded, and the shortcut turns into a cul-de-sac. Therefore, there are no easy roads or shortcuts in this world. Until now,

I haven't had the good fortune of having the easy road and the shortcut appear briefly in my life.

Profits yielded through corrupt means aren't profits, but debts. Debts must be repaid someday, and it is natural that our children will be forced to repay them if we don't. Debt will tenaciously find its way in the form of compound interest. I hope you won't doubt that conscientiousness and honesty are the most right and proper paths, and that you will have faith as you follow the flow of life.

52

Weaknesses Become Strengths When Disclosed

My wife's nickname when she was young was 'white fox'.[16] It's a nickname that women with the surname Baek will have heard at least once in their lives. It wasn't exactly a swear word, but she detested it, because it wasn't a pleasant nickname either. She also detested being called a white fox herself. That nickname was my wife's Achilles heel. The reason is that a white fox is regarded on an almost equal footing with a white vixen, a shrew, or the legendary fox with nine tails.[17] But I translated into English the phrase 'white fox', which has a negative connotation, and used it as a brand name. I knew it would remain a nickname if it were uttered only by some, but that it would instead create a sense of friendliness and thereby become a term of endearment if it were uttered by many people.

---

16 Translator's note: The phrase 'white fox' is a translation from the Korean *baek* (white) *yeowoo* (fox).

17 Translator's note: In Korean folk culture, foxes are typically used to symbolise women, while wolves, tigers and dragons symbolise men. Other animals that are used to symbolise women include snakes and cats. This contrast suggests that women are subordinate to men and embody malevolent qualities such as craftiness and malice.

There are a few English phrases to describe a white fox. I passed over 'Arctic fox', a common name for foxes living near the North Pole, because its pronunciation wasn't smooth, and someone else had already registered 'polar fox', so the phrase that remained was... SnowFox. It's a term that is easy to pronounce, whose image is easy to recall, and which is translated directly from the Korean word for white fox. When our brand became widely known and our logo was publicised, people who wanted the nickname 'white fox' showed up – although they weren't female employees from our company with the surname Baek. As more people came to like the name SnowFox, my wife's mortification morphed into pride, and she no longer detested being called a white fox.

There are many opportunities to transform weaknesses into strengths by disclosing them. When South Korean comedian Joo-Il Lee spoke openly about his ugliness, his looks became likeable. The biggest weakness of a leader is the attitude that refuses to acknowledge one's weaknesses. It's a given that a person is unable to outshine others in every respect. When we nevertheless emphasise our brilliance, people in our midst who would come to our aid will vanish, and those who will obstruct us show up instead. A leader isn't someone who has outstanding abilities; a leader is defined by the extent to which they can assemble people around them who will make up for their inadequacies.

The most powerful person isn't someone who is authoritative or wealthy. The most powerful person is someone who has many friends around them who will help them and pray for their success. And when they become known as someone who openly acknowledges their own weaknesses and seeks help, respect for them will increase. Small leaders are garrulous and often patronising, but those who aspire to be big leaders listen a great deal to others and know full well that seeking help doesn't lower but increases their worth.

Even if we refuse to consider our weaknesses as weaknesses, disclosing them is the only way to gain favour with others in this world. The music of a person who sings a song earnestly to the end, without knowing that they are tone deaf, has achieved just that.

'As more people came to like the name SnowFox, my wife's mortification morphed into pride, and she no longer detested being called a white fox.'

53

Thirteen Differences Between the Successful and the Hugely Successful

There are obvious differences between novice and veteran CEOs, those who have recently succeeded and those who continue to succeed, wealthy people worth $1 billion and those worth $10 billion or $100 billion. They have all succeeded, but their successes are different, and their differences form the criteria through which we can evaluate how much further they can progress.

1. **Those who have succeeded for the first time think they have succeeded by their own abilities, but those who have achieved huge successes think of them as good fortune.** Hugely successful individuals are prudent and not conceited when they succeed on one occasion, because they know their successes aren't recurrent. Conversely, those who have succeeded for the first time instantly push ahead with excessive investments and risks to achieve a second success, and easily end up ruining themselves.

2. **Successful individuals build and sell their companies, but hugely successful individuals keep their companies till the day they die.** Hugely successful individuals know it wouldn't be easy to discover other better businesses with the money they received from selling their own company. They therefore devote all their energies to sustaining their present business so that it will last a lifetime. This is

because they can't find an area for investment that will yield as much profit as their own companies have done by using money received from selling their possessions.

3. **Successful people work twenty hours a day, but hugely successful people work only eight hours.** Successful people work numerous hours to save on payroll expenses. They think the more they work till late in the evening, the more they can lower employees' payroll. However, hugely successful people can balance family, personal life and work, because they know the method of calculating payroll expenses based on profits yielded per business rather than per hour. Therefore, they work early in the morning and end work early.

4. **Successful people sustain growth with rules and regulations, but hugely successful people succeed by transcending them.** When a company expands, diverse employees join the organisation, and regulations are needed to govern them. But these regulations make both the organisation and thinking rigid, and become as destructive as a double-edged sword. Those who have achieved bigger successes therefore understand the initial purpose of setting rules and regulations, and keep them in check.

5. **Successful individuals learn from their seniors, but hugely successful individuals from their juniors.** The success stories of our seniors can never be applied to us in the same way. And our juniors offer fresh perspectives.

6. **Successful individuals watch their own companies, but those who seek bigger successes keep their eyes on the industry.** A company resembles a branch or leaf of an industry. We can't see that the whole tree is experiencing a drought if we are preoccupied only with the company's sustainability or growth.

7. **Successful people are fond of research and planning, but hugely successful people believe in intuition and discernment.** Market

research is more pointless than we think. This is because consumers themselves have no idea what they want. If a business is built on planning and research, it will be operated like a mathematical formula. The fact that there hasn't been a business formula thus far suggests that intuition and discernment are still significant forces at work.

8. **Successful people are preoccupied with defeating competitors, but hugely successful people work hard to triumph over themselves.** We are our own biggest competitor in the world. When we attempt to diet, we soon realise how much effort is needed to triumph over ourselves. And we realise how terrifying a competitor we are.

9. **Successful people are busy battling competitors within their fences, but hugely successful people are also vigilant of competitors who seek to enter by boring through the fences.** Who knew that the automobile industry would be kept on its toes by Google, or be caught unawares by Apple's bridle over them? Industry competitors today no longer cross over fences; they fly through them.

10. **Successful individuals rely on memory, but hugely successful individuals trust memos and records.** Memory isn't facts. Memory is fabricated, altered and forgotten. Records alone preserve facts.

11. **Successful individuals possess things, but hugely successful individuals possess cash.** Successful individuals purchase and collect things such as jewellery, houses, cars and luxury products that will depreciate and disappear, but hugely successful individuals purchase and collect things such as properties and company shares that will yield profits.

12. **Successful people are highly interested in saving money, but hugely successful people are highly interested in making money.** The costs of managing and supervising certain tasks for the sake of cutting back on small expenses often far outweigh the sum of money

saved. Hugely successful people therefore deliberate instead over ways to make more money in the same period.

13. **Successful people live beyond their means, but hugely successful people live below their means.** Successful people desire to construct evidence to display their success. Hugely successful people construct lives in which they can live as comfortably as possible, because they know that even after boasting of their success, they could still lose everything they have because of a small blunder.

Part 5

Let's Be Kind and Faithful, But Shrewd and Indolent

Not everything in this world can be forgiven because one is kind and faithful. We must be kind and faithful, and simultaneously shrewd and indolent. We can shield kindness with shrewdness, and only by desiring to be indolent can we manage our work wisely. We have many strengths that only become strengths alongside our other strong points. Being kind and faithful are two of them.

54

The Mistakes and Megalomania of
Intelligent People

Humans' average IQ is 100. This is how IQ standards have been determined. Humans' average IQ has been set at 100, irrespective of age. Therefore, sixty-eight percent of the world's population fall into the IQ range of 85 to 150. But many people joke about whether someone resembles a monkey if their IQ is around 90. People usually think we need a score of around 130 to be normal. The fact is, given the margin of error, not only will there not be a significant difference between 90 and 110, but 100 is also perfectly normal because it lies right at the centre of the world's scores.

I believe that people with an IQ of 100 have the best brains for doing business. When I look at my entrepreneur peers, they don't seem to belong to the group of people with especially high IQ. Come to think of it, intelligent people have a few habits that aren't suitable for doing business. One of them is playing the megalomaniac detective who makes judgements based on their own deductions – which they overrate, because they believe that their assumptions are never wrong.

They believe their friend has a kept woman simply because when they meet him by chance there is a woman standing beside him who lowers her head without greeting them. They are certain the couple has a house in the vicinity because the woman is dressed casually and standing outside a shop in the evening. Their friend's wife – who hasn't exchanged greetings simply because she is embarrassed to be seen without make-up – has become a kept woman two weeks later.

When orders from their business partners decrease only slightly, they think their partners are going to stop partnering them, or they worry that this has happened because they didn't welcome them warmly when they last visited. They are hugely conscious of people's criticisms and sentiments. Diverse speculations unfold endlessly, one after the other. But many people aren't as interested in you as you think.

Occasionally, there are instances where people kill themselves after being implicated in scandalous incidents and becoming the talk of the town. They presume that everyone on earth will mock them, and they resort to extreme measures. However, these scandals are incidents the general public will have forgotten the next day.

Being intelligent and being wise are obviously different. I believe that intelligent people possess good analytical abilities and good memories, and can make better judgements than people with an IQ of 100. But wisdom doesn't come from IQ alone. Wisdom is manifested when we learn to empathise with the feelings of the other party or the people around us. A common cause is formed when we empathise with the people around us, and we are in accord when we understand this common cause.

After all, a business doesn't grow by being extraordinary; it grows by maintaining unchanging values.

55

Money Is a Person

Most people spend the majority of their time in their lives making money. The biggest concern of those who are currently engaged in economic activity is: how can I make money? That said, there is something people are often mistaken about.

Usually, when humans categorise their thoughts, they tend to dichotomise them into the psychological and the material, and this is when they consider money to be the archetype of material things. I suppose the difference between those who can and those who can't make money begins here. We mustn't think of money as a purely material thing, but as a person.

Money is a person. Money too has life. When we laugh at the coins that fall out of our pockets and don't pick them up, treat them thoughtlessly as petty cash, or spend large sums on unjustified items without hesitation, it's an affront to a person called money. Coins are children, and large sums of money are adults. Is there anyone who likes people who treat their children recklessly? Money doesn't see any reason to revisit such people. This is because money feels hurt.

When a person cherishes money, spends it in the right places and handles it appropriately, money will certainly like that person, bring along other friends, and stay forever.

We are attracted to people who appreciate and treat us appropriately, and we want to see and be with them. Money is also the product of circumstances produced by certain behaviours.

All behaviours in this world are connected. This applies not only to interactions between living things; it's a phenomenon that happens similarly with intangible things, non-living things and our thoughts. When someone is unduly infatuated with money, money grows weary of that love and takes flight. When someone is unduly oblivious of money, money ignores them and stays away. Money longs to return to someone who saves it when they should and spends it willingly in good places. I hope you will therefore think of money as a person with a personality.

56

The Differences Between Frugality and Miserliness

One of the common mistakes that CEOs make is not being able to differentiate between frugality and miserliness. Conserving electricity is frugality. But clothing employees with thick clothes and then reducing the use of heaters is miserliness. Buying a simple meal for yourself is frugality, but feeding employees cheap food is miserliness. CEOs are unable to differentiate between frugality and miserliness when they dress themselves in inexpensive clothes and then pressure employees into living in the same manner, or present themselves as role models in life.

Frugality should be restricted to oneself. It's no longer business but religion when we force it on or teach it to our family, employees or anyone. It's great to be self-controlled and frugal without boasting about our wealth. But in every respect, this behaviour should stop at our own actions. Misers don't know that they are miserly. Most of them are very frugal and personally consider their frugality a virtue. However, frugality morphs into miserliness the instant one demands this frugality of others.

A person becomes a miser when frugality is no longer restricted to themselves. When you attend a company dinner with your employees, you shouldn't order *jjajangmyeon* first, even if it's more delicious than *tangsooyook*. You should order only after all your employees have ordered, and order *palbochae* even if you wish to have *jjajangmyeon*.[18] And when the *palbochae* arrives, you can share it with the employees who ordered *jjajangmyeon*. A CEO isn't a teacher but merely a leader of an organisation called a company. A CEO can play the adult role when making business decisions with employees, but it's unreasonable to do the same outside work. When a CEO doesn't recognise this, they will boast about their own frugality and impose it on employees. Employees who work for such CEOs will meddle with company assets as a way of dealing with miserly bosses, and will ditch their allegiance when the opportunity arises.

Even if a CEO drives a small car, they shouldn't ask employees to help them get a bigger one, or reproach employees for driving big cars. This is because every employee has different life goals, and their motivations for working in the company are obviously different from the CEO's. We can become great leaders when we recognise that frugality turns into miserliness the instant we no longer restrict the practice to ourselves, but if we don't recognise this fact and the situation worsens, no one will stay by our side.

18 Translator's note: *Palbochae* is a dish that combines eight ingredients, including vegetables and seafood. It is typically far more expensive than *jjajangmyeon*, a noodle dish topped with black bean sauce and diced pork and vegetables, or *tangsooyook*, a fried meat dish with sweet and sour sauce.

57

Heaven Is Here

If you hold religious beliefs that anticipate a beautiful world after death, I have a piece of good news for you. You can go there even without having to die.

Everyone longs to be happy. And because this happiness can't be fulfilled in this world, we have faith in an afterlife and set our sights on heaven. But I have positive evidence that heaven is nothing compared with our lives on earth. Among all my friends who are interested in spirituality, including pastors, no one wants to die today. We are always worried about how we can increase our income, by however little, we take nutritional supplements, and we are certain to fasten our seat belts when we drive. I had a friend who said it didn't matter if he couldn't go to heaven as long as he could play golf every day. No one wants to go to that beautiful heaven quickly.

It's clear what this implies. Even for people with strong religious faith, the world we are currently living in is far better than an uncertain future. In that case, heaven is here. If the countless believers were given a choice between dying right now and living in this world forever, heaven would be entirely empty. I believe heaven is the world we are now inhabiting. We are now in heaven. But it's simply our individual choice whether we turn this place into heaven or not. I also believe the lifespan of humans has been set so that we can impart this idea to others and feel the nobility of this heaven.

It's indescribably regrettable to see people who have no idea that heaven is here now, who set their sights on heaven after death, who despise the position they are now in and recklessly waste their lives. I see countless people spending their time here in heaven lying on the couch with bags of crisps, playing games or squandering their money on alcohol, ruining each day meaninglessly. It seems the heavens haven't told these people, who are ruining every day they have been given, that heaven is here, because they don't wish to bestow heaven on them.

Work hard and study hard. Love with all your heart, share friendships, comfort those who are hurt, participate in society, vote, have fun, and try to participate in an artistic activity. Grow flowers or vegetables, and raise animals. Leave marks in life so that those who survive you when you really leave this world will miss the times they have spent with you as times spent in heaven.

The moment we think that religions generally espouse pure, unblemished truths, we grow distant from the truths they wish to proclaim. I have no way of explaining the heaven of this world, which I have just described, to people who still consider the heaven they will go to after death to be the destination of perfect happiness. But when people who highly value this life – which we live only once – comprehend what I mean by 'heaven is here', they will realise that they are living in heaven right now.

As soon as you feel urgently that this life doesn't come twice, your heaven on earth will begin right away.

58

No One Has Got Rich by Diversifying Investments

One of the commonest investing methods recommended by people who advise on asset management is diversified investing. Diversifying investments to minimise risks is a classic way of investing. But let's think this over. Has anyone got rich by diversifying investments?

Let's say you run a restaurant. Do you produce menus that incorporate Korean food, Japanese food and Chinese food equally because you don't know what customers in a small-scale shopping district will want? You wish to start a business. Will you start a convenience store and a print shop and take over a bookshop because you have no idea which business will pan out well? No. If you wish to run a business, won't you spend several years learning about that specific business, and accrue experience in the business world before giving your all to operate it to the utmost? Why do we operate businesses in this way, but diversify when we invest our money?

The idea that diversifying investments reduces risks means there will be no chance of getting rich. Moreover, if we feel tempted to diversify investments, it is evidence that we don't have one hundred percent confidence in any of those diversified investment areas. There is a time when diversifying investments is useful. That is when you are already wealthy, and protecting your wealth becomes a bigger goal. We can never join the ranks of wealthy people with our salaries and savings alone. Among those who have become massively wealthy, I haven't seen a single person who has amassed wealth by diversifying investments. Wealthy people are people who have succeeded in their businesses despite having had scarce opportunities, or who have made massive profits through speculatively inclined investments. When we stow our eggs in various places because we worry they might crack if they are all placed in one basket, it's easy to forget where we have put them.

The stock market is where this theory of diversified investing receives the most support. People in the securities industry advise us to split shares, which we have researched and are eligible for investing, into multiple shares and to purchase them. However, even blue-chip shares pose risks, and their prices don't all increase evenly, although they are shares we have researched. The more intriguing thing is that even people who work in the stock market aren't one hundred percent confident that the share prices will increase. If they were confident, they would have already acquired the shares using their entire fortune and financial leverage, and they would now be ready to retire.

How should we invest, if we shouldn't diversify our investments or heed the advice of employees in securities companies? The answer is simple. If you wish to acquire a company's shares, even if it's just one share, act as if you have resolved to acquire the entire company. Peruse the company's ledger, visit the company, and meet with relevant employees. You shouldn't invest in their shares if they retort 'What is all the fuss about if you are only buying a few shares?' or if you don't have the time or even the confidence to do it. You should put in everything you have and wait, but only when you are truly fond of a company you have researched and you are bent on sticking with it for the rest of your life. Don't you think you would be very prudent with your decisions if the government made it legal for a person to buy and sell shares only five times in a lifetime? Once you have prudently chosen a company, you can place all your investment money according to your preference.

Now I have confidence and assurance in my investments. This is because I know every detail about the company I have chosen, more than employees from securities companies. I am fully aware of the company's new product releases, changes in management, and its progress in dominating the market. I am also fully aware of the differences in profit ratios between this quarter and the last, or other quarters in the previous year. The reason is that this company may be only one of many others whose shares are traded by stockbrokers, but it's *my* company.

The best way to invest in order to join the ranks of wealthy individuals has a speculative element. It involves discovering an area for investment where we can make a huge fortune at one stroke, and willingly placing everything we have on the line. A considerable number of experts will feel aversion towards this investment method, and will reject it with all sorts of reasoning. The fascinating thing is that none of the experts who dismiss this method is a truly wealthy person.

Self-made wealthy people are shareholders in companies which have withstood imprudent real-estate investments and ridicule, and succeeded in being listed; and they are company CEOs who have risked their entire fortunes and families and succeeded, even when they saw only a one percent chance of success. People like them (I don't know if they themselves are aware of this, but it is true of all of them) are individuals who have succeeded in concentrated speculative investments. Therefore, if you truly aspire to amass massive wealth among people who aren't likely to be wealthy, discover something that is worth concentrating on, and pour your fortune and efforts into it. We can't become truly wealthy people without such valour and audacity. We can only buy lottery tickets and wait till our elderly parents get rich.

59

Horoscopes, Blood Types and Multilevel Marketing

I keep a wide berth of people who earnestly believe that the fates or personalities of humankind are differentiated according to horoscopes and blood types, as well as people who are experienced in multilevel marketing. I don't wish to promote employees who hold such beliefs, and I feel I can't interact seriously with such friends around me as soon as I realise that they believe in these things. This is because it shows how ignorant they are of a person's potential and the variability of the personality.

Our fates vary with the magnitude of our thoughts and the trajectories we take, and it's ludicrous that human personalities are divided into just a few blood types. Multilevel marketing is a somewhat different story, but it's one of the most underhand ways of making money by turning everyone we know into business avenues, including people with whom we have delicate and beautiful relationships, from our close family to other relatives and friends. Understanding a person's potential and variability is the start of love. There is value in human existence only when we have become better human beings after meeting a person. Those who consider this value to be a moneymaking opportunity are truly pitiable.

When Daniel was eighteen, he starved for three days, then crossed the Mexican border into the United States. One day, at a job market in a car park, I caught sight of him, blended into a crowd of people searching for jobs, dressed neatly in a clean cap. I liked how he stood upright, without leaning against the wall as the others did, as he looked for people who might give him a job, so I brought him back with me. Now we have been working together for ten years and he has become a healthy young man.

Daniel, who married at the age of seventeen and has a wife and a child, returned to his hometown two years ago. A native of a rural Mexican village where the daily wage was below $2, he had already remitted $30,000 to his father to purchase a house and a piece of land, so it was a glorious return, and he became a celebrated young man whom many called a millionaire. When he returned to work, he did everything independently, tirelessly and readily as though it was all part of his job, he was invariably cheerful, and everyone who worked with him was pleased.

Extract from *Note on Self-Management*

60

The Worst Wife, the Worst Employee

The hardest-to-live-with wife on earth is a kind wife, and the hardest-to-manage employee is a conscientious employee. This isn't paradoxical. Humble people don't consider themselves humble, but kind people know that they are kind.

A kind wife makes sacrifices for her husband and children, and always prepares more than is needed. She is meek and bears no grudges. Then, gradually, this gives rise to a compensation mentality. As soon as she realises that she hasn't been and won't be treated well or compensated by her children or husband, now or in the future, compared with all that she has sacrificed, she begins to exercise her power. I call this power obstinacy. And this obstinacy doesn't come with fixed rules; it manifests itself unpredictably.

She enforces the consumption of multigrain rice, irrespective of individual preferences, or she shifts every computer in the entire household into the living room. She doesn't do this without a reason. Her reason is to keep her sons, who run off to their individual rooms, in the living room for the sake of the family's health and harmony. However, using her family as a pretext, she instructs and requires her children and husband to adhere to numerous rules because of trivial small decisions she has made.

There are two reasons for these behaviours. One is resistance, through which she intends to do as she pleases because she is a victim; and the other is her presumption that she is acting in good faith for the good of everyone, because she is always a kind person. These women don't heed advice or recommendations from people around them. Because they are very kind women. They think they are right because they are kind. Husbands and children who have kind wives and mothers are unable to find anyone who understands or sympathises with them. Husbands know that their siblings and parents live comfortably thanks to their kind wives. But their families can hardly breathe.

Conscientious employees can be a bane in the office. I once instructed an employee to collect pamphlets from every company that was participating in an exhibition. Two hours would have sufficed, but by closing time he still hadn't shown up. There were only a few pamphlets in the hands of the employee when he finally showed up late. When I asked why, he said collecting pamphlets alone didn't seem helpful to the company, so he had listened to every company introduce all of their products. He showed me his notebook, which was filled with written notes. Thanks to him, we had to attend the event until the next day.

Once, we planned to introduce a newly launched product to a partner company. I instructed that this product should be delivered to that company through a nearby branch office. I sent the branch office manager, as it was an important matter. I instructed him to only deliver the product to a company executive at a scheduled time, and to remain tight-lipped about the product and our company. I didn't want to cause any confusion, as our marketing team was still ironing out the details. But the manager, whose fervour got the better of him, made the mistake of handing out his business card and introducing himself as the manager of that region. The executive then requested a detailed introduction to the product, and flooded him with questions about pricing and follow-up services. Before the marketing team from headquarters had even arrived, the meeting, which had been difficult to arrange, had fallen apart. Later, when I pressed the manager for his reason, he explained he had wanted to introduce himself and become more closely acquainted with the executive beforehand, because he would be overseeing that company if the deal had panned out well.

When problems cropped up in a store located two hours away, the ever-zealous manager travelled back and forth several times a day to demonstrate his conscientiousness. But his superiors perceived the store's mishaps as problems that could have been avoided beforehand. In the end, he was zealous about resolving problems that had occurred because of his own lack of management. He spent company funds needlessly as a result, but on the other hand he obviously desired to be praised for his zeal. He boasted about his own conscientiousness right up until the moment he was dismissed, but from management's standpoint he was merely someone who had conscientiously caused trouble.

Not everything in this world can be forgiven because one is being kind and faithful. We must be kind and faithful, and simultaneously shrewd and indolent. We can shield kindness with shrewdness, and only by desiring to be indolent can we manage our work wisely. We have many strengths that only become strengths alongside our other strong points. Being kind and faithful are two of them.

61

My Reasons for Making Money

I have two rather obvious and clear reasons for making money. The first is to provide for my family. For a man and head of a household, providing for one's family is the most practical reason.

I feel satisfied and proud when I spend the money I have made on protecting my family, and on their well-being. Some people are worried that excessive love for one's family will produce a society in which citizens are shut off from activities outside the family, and that their rights and freedoms will deteriorate because of this disinterest in social activities. But it isn't just about providing for my own family; I believe this sense of responsibility for providing for my family can even promote social justice.

There will be people who have fathers that are very miserly with their own families but exceedingly generous with other people. What will remain for children who grow up with such fathers and their wives is merely a reputation for being superficially envied for having such wonderful fathers, and debt securities. These fathers feel rewarded and find value in life when they use their fortune, time and talents on others. They are strict with themselves and magnanimous with others. It's clearly a virtue to be strict with oneself and magnanimous with others. But problems arise because these fathers equate their families with themselves. They should draw a clear distinction between themselves and their families. This is because their wives and children are independent individuals first before they are family members.

It's better to do good for our country before doing good for humankind, and better to do good for our local community before doing good for our country. If it's difficult to do good for our local community, we should first do good for our relatives and friends, and of course our close family comes before our friends and other relatives. Depending on your abilities, be responsible for your close family members first, and if you can still afford it, take care of your relatives and friends, then your local community and your country. I think we should first take care of starving African children before we boil eggs for our puppies and feed them beef, and we should first check on starving children in the house behind ours before we care for children in another country several thousand miles away.

I hope that the people around me, including my family, will be the first to benefit from the money I make. I must first satisfy my close family, other relatives, employees and friends. I shouldn't endow a scholarship at an outstanding university if my niece is unable to attend school. My company shouldn't donate tens of thousands of dollars to the local community if our employees' salaries aren't satisfactory. It's natural that water flows from top to bottom.

My second reason for making money is to buy time in my life. I have but one life. I can't buy two lives or own three with the money I have made, but money helps me do what I wish to do with the time I have been given. It's great that more money can be made as my business expands, but this leads to a vicious cycle in which I must spend more time on the business to make a great deal of money.

A CEO's busyness isn't a matter of the magnitude of work, but their mental attitude. A CEO is in a position where they can be as busy or as free as they desire. There is a way to obtain results by working busily, but there is also a way to obtain better results without having to do that.

A CEO who constantly interferes with and manages the business because they are doubtful about delegating authority to someone else is unable to live their life, no matter how much the business has grown. We can't even berate them if work is their life goal. However, if we aren't born for the sake of operating a company, we should work in a way that doesn't require us to work. Delegate authority and responsibilities to your subordinates. And trust them. If you can't, make yourself believe that you trust them. Everyone loves to work for people who recognise their worth and trust them.

The more people you trust, the freer you become. Your freedom is your worth. The freedom to earn a livelihood without working for others is the high spot of business. Providing for my family and having perfect freedom in life – as an entrepreneur, these are the qualities of which I am proudest, and which are the most deserving of respect.

62

A CEO Should Be Healthy

People believe they can make their bodies healthy and lose weight by dieting. But a person's body doesn't change with intermittent dieting. It simply pretends to change. It will only bounce back fast, like a ball thrown at a wall. All dieting makes weight loss possible by controlling food intake, but we completely return to our former selves when the dieting ends.

A person's body is a product that reflects their lifestyle. Dieting can't effect positive change in our body because it's a temporary thing. If you resolve to lose weight by dieting or exercising, you should focus on a sustainable activity. If you plan to diet, you should improve your diet by focusing on eating habits that can last a lifetime, and if you plan to exercise, you should consider exercises you can do throughout the rest of your life. If you aren't confident of keeping up with your current exercises or diets for the rest of your life, you will obtain the same results whether you quit now or later. Therefore, the best way is to decide on habits that can last a lifetime without a hitch, and to incorporate them into your lifestyle – habits such as refraining from snacking between meals instead of going on a sudden diet, consuming water instead of carbonated drinks, consuming less sugar and fat, and walking and taking the stairs whenever possible.

The goal of dieting and exercise is a healthy body. Our minds change when our bodies change, and our bodies change when our minds change. When many good habits enter our lives, our backs are straightened, our abdominal fat disappears, our buttocks are lifted, and our complexion becomes smoother. A body gained from forced dieting or immoderate exercise will eventually only be defeated by our habits. If you wish to commit to dieting, I strongly advise you to start by figuring out lifestyle habits that can last a lifetime.

We are, after all, the product of our everyday lifestyle habits. What we eat shapes us, and our habits form who we are. Being overweight means our diets and habits aren't formed right. When we are sensible about life, and there is no excess or imbalance in our diets, we will have the most impressive body we can possibly have. There is no need to worry about dieting. Having the right eating habits and the right attitudes in life is the most effective diet.

63

Bad Customers

You will meet bad customers when you work in the service industry. There will be occasions when they ride roughshod over employees, display violent behaviour or demand excessive service. There will also be occasions when they make unreasonable demands or are disrespectful towards other customers. We tolerate these behaviours because they have paid and are considered customers no matter what they do. These customers think that people who are provided with a service are superior to those who provide the service. But it's a fair transaction to pay for a service that has been provided. This transaction doesn't include personal insults or disrespectful behaviour, let alone behaviour that inconveniences other customers.

A transaction is a fair affair. It's simply an exchange between service and payment. But disrespectful customers are under the illusion that customers can do anything they please. Customers are treated as customers only when they display the dignity that befits a customer. To demand undue compensation when employees commit minor mistakes, to speak harshly, or to bring along children and leave them unattended are all behaviours that overstep the rights of customers. Abusive language and violence are obvious. In developed countries, businesses have the right to refuse service to such customers.

I have given our employees discretionary power to refuse such customers. In particular, customers who intimidate or inconvenience other customers are permanently banned from entering our stores. We are businesspeople, not philanthropists. Our service doesn't include or sell products that incorporate self-sacrifice. It's also an executive's responsibility to construct an environment in which employees can provide a sincere service. This is the rightful and respectful reception that excellent customers deserve. However, in order to uphold our business policy regarding bad customers, we should also recognise when we are someone else's customers, and behave appropriately.

We are customers to our partners and subcontractors. We should be excellent customers to them. We should always inspect products and pay for them at the same time. We should also be grateful that they are trading with us. The 'there are other places I can buy from besides them' attitude is the same as the one we hear from our customers: 'Do you think there are no other stores apart from yours?'

Customers say thank you even when they are shopping in supermarkets in the United States. There are numerous instances when shop assistants reply simply 'You are welcome', rather than 'Don't mention it. We are grateful'. This implies that service and payment are exchanged equally. Likewise, we should also show equal respect to all the wholesalers, manufacturers, financiers, store owners, delivery persons and so on who supply us with products and services. I hope we will respect our customers without being servile, and increase our value by expressing gratitude and respect to service providers when we are the customers.

64

How Extravagant Should Wealthy People Be?

Yang is seen, and *yin* is unseen. A person who can afford to be as extravagant as they desire but chooses not to has a remarkably fine character. However, there are several occasions when we should wield the *yang* character if we wish to do business. This is not like boasting. It's like not being able to enter the second floor of a shabbily run-down bank building, or a conglomerate not being able to operate its business because its office premises are built on an unpaved car park inside a makeshift building in a field. The reason is that a building's size and form impact a business's credibility and its present and future value. This applies to people too. We can deduce a person's credibility and present value by their appearance, car, clothes and accessories.

I once attended a food exhibition in Tokyo with a few people I was meeting for the first time. Before we had introduced ourselves, I couldn't guess at all what their professions were. It wasn't a matter of frugality. When one of them, who was wearing a short-sleeved T-shirt bought from a market, a pair of knee-length shorts and well-worn shoes, introduced himself as the CEO of a newspaper company, it didn't matter exactly which newspaper it was – I already had a preconceived idea of how the company looked.

An entrepreneur should dress neatly and properly, consistent with the scale of their business and fitting for their business partners. Shoes should be immaculate, shirts pressed, jackets and trousers smart-looking. Luxury products without logos are good too.

Buy your wife the best car, but buy a similar car for yourself if you can afford it. It's good to purchase the best house within the bounds of the debt you can shoulder, and to buy it in your wife's name. A company is a reward and symbol for a CEO, while a house and car mean the same things to a spouse. We shouldn't neglect to wield and exhibit the *yang* character on the pretext of simplicity. Our clothes are used to convey politeness towards and respect for the other party, and because it also expresses authority, it's good if we are dressed elegantly without appearing boastful.

However, we should be extremely cautious and self-controlled about eating problems that possess the *yin* character. We shouldn't splurge on exorbitant food, we should never binge eat or overeat, and we should mend the habit of eating at irregular hours. We shouldn't spend more than is needed. We shouldn't drink to the point of inebriation, and we should distance ourselves from everything to which we could become addicted. We should be wealthy in appearance but poor at heart. Only then can we amass more wealth and positively influence more people.

You are never alone when the world transforms you into a wealthy person. Every thought and life in this world have helped you out, and your behaviour and circumstances were formed in the meanwhile so you could obtain this wealth. Your stylish houses, cars and beautiful clothes – the products of your business – will all disappear the moment you eat irregularly, binge eat and overeat. The amount of food you should eat throughout your life, from the day you were born, has been set. Therefore, you will perish quickly if you eat quickly, but if you use food gratefully, a little at a time, you will live a long and healthy life, and nothing you have that possesses the *yang* character will crumble away.

It's appalling to think about how much more food people dump into their bellies than is needed. All food has life. The world's harmony will no longer come to your aid if you recklessly turn life into excrement. The gods you serve won't be pleased about this. It isn't just food; paper, pencils, wastepaper and desks were originally living things. We ought to cherish and respect all of them. When a wealthy person learns to do that, they learn the beginning and end of life. I hope that people whose businesses have always foundered despite thriving initially, and those who are ill for no reason, will examine their eating habits and learn to respect everything that has life. Then they will never fail and will live to a healthy old age.

65

The Seemingly Irrelevant But Essential Matters in Business

Among those who have suddenly built a business or succeeded by their own efforts, sometimes there are people who haven't acquired an entrepreneur's basic etiquette. There may be instances when they don't have a senior beside them to sternly point that out to them, or when they don't feel the need to have one. Or perhaps they are relaxed, hoping to be appreciated for their unique personalities. However, just as we receive a public education when we enrol in nursery school, so we ought to learn public etiquette if we wish to excel in our role as a CEO. The sooner we receive this basic education, the better. The reason is that people perceive a person's greatness and lowliness in the minor things. The following is a list of basic rules of etiquette. I wish to specify them because we can't recognise them if we don't meticulously and frankly make them known.

- Always keep your shoes clean.
- Always trim your moustache and nasal hair.
- Clean your ears, and keep earwax out of sight.
- Keep your nails short, and be careful not to dirty them.
- Comb your hair neatly.
- Clean yourself up with tissues while eating.
- Do not shake your legs.

- Do not sit hunched.
- Do not eat hurriedly or leave crumbs on the table.

Shoes reflect a person's attitude in life. We look poor, destitute and somehow disordered when our shoes are covered with dirt or creased. When our shoes are dirty, we are bound to appear as somehow untrustworthy people.

We don't have to clean our shoes once a week, but I recommend cleaning them as frequently as necessary, and to always clean them before you go out and stand in them before someone you are meeting for the first time. When we clean our shoes before we go out in them, it is an expression of etiquette and respect for the other party.

There are manners that women are strict about. Once, I was introduced to a new lawyer in a law firm. I saw some hair at the base of his neck that hadn't been trimmed in a long time, and a few strands of nasal hair bundled together and sticking out of his nose. The women who had attended the meeting with me weren't interested in the lawyer's impressive background. They simply wanted the meeting to conclude quickly. None of the people who had seen him wanted to see him again, so no one wanted to give him any work.

When men shave, they sometimes shave only the visible parts. We must check if our beard is growing long under our chin, and always be wary of nasal hair, because many people show an extreme reaction to nasal hair that borders on disgust. An outcrop of earwax and ear hair disgust people too. We aren't perceived as experts when our nails are dirty; we should be cautious of leaving food stains in the corners of our mouth, even when we are sitting opposite our lover, because this is considered cute only until the age of ten; we appear frivolous when we shake our legs in front of adults; we appear to lack confidence when we sit hunched; we give the impression that we are financially insecure or being hounded when we eat hurriedly.

I hope that when we adhere to the points above, we show ourselves to be authoritative and dignified in the eyes of our subordinates, as well as respectful and polite in the eyes of our elders, and thereby do not ruin ourselves through minor shortcomings.

66

If You Wish to Gain the Other Party's Respect

I once met an American entrepreneur. He was a young entrepreneur who owned a wonderful business after succeeding single-handedly amid gruelling circumstances. I had heard he operated his company like clockwork, and I met him to learn the peculiar characteristics of his management style – purely as friends, rather than as a business meeting.

After we had exchanged greetings, introduced ourselves (this was our first meeting) and looked around his company, we sat face-to-face in his office. He started to candidly unpack his life story to an outsider. He must have wanted to boast. His story of hitting rock bottom before rising again was as riveting as a tale of fiction. His business was a feather in his cap and was being operated adroitly, just as I had heard. However, as I listened on, I wanted to blow my own trumpet, and the words 'That's nothing' repeatedly rose to my lips. But I had reread Dale Carnegie's *How to Win Friends and Influence People* a while before on my way to the office, so I simply held back. The meeting, which I had thought would last an hour, exceeded three hours. I had no idea whether he liked me – I didn't once interrupt him, and I asked questions and listened to all that he said – but he appeared immensely relieved once he had finished speaking. Perhaps I was the first person to have listened so intently to his personal story.

He said everything he wanted to say. I didn't wish to take the bloom off his moving achievements with my own story, which came second to his, and I didn't want to discourage him by revealing my company size in response to his boasting about his own company's size. As a prideful person, I did want to take him down a peg or two, but I decided to stick to Carnegie's teachings, and I wrapped up the meeting.

A month later, I met him again at a meeting with several entrepreneurs. I worried that he would emanate the same haughtiness as on that day, but my worries were unfounded. He dragged me hither and thither to everyone in the meeting, and started to boast about how excellent a person I was and how I was one of the people he respected most. We weren't such close friends and hadn't known each other long enough for me to be respected by him, but the pride and haughtiness he had shown me on our first meeting had been expunged entirely, and it seemed I was piggybacking on him. Everyone found it odd that he, who had an exceptionally strong boss-like temperament, was behaving in this way. The only thing I had done for him was listen while he talked.

That day I learned an important lesson. The person who asks and listens in a conversation is superior to the person who talks and responds to questions. How many times do we long to object, justify ourselves, or take the lead in a conversation? Although we know these methods always fail to gain the other party's respect, we are impatient to explain ourselves and are busy getting others to understand us, habitually cutting in when someone is speaking, or wandering from the core of a conversation to talk about something else.

On days when I talk a lot, I realise I have erred by the end of the evening. I am exceptionally cautious, especially when conversing with people I am befriending for the first time, but I can't completely obliterate my arrogance. On days when I return home after bragging about myself or needlessly pretending to be a know-it-all, I begin to quietly feel embarrassed by evening. We are bound to err when we talk too much, and we are bound to boast when we talk too much. I don't know why I keep forgetting that simply listening and asking questions is effortless, and by doing it I can gain the other party's respect.

67

Growing at Forty, Stopping at Forty

There are people who start growing at the age of forty, and people who stop growing at the age of forty. People stop growing at forty if they succeed before the age of forty, and they start growing at forty if they succeed after the age of forty. There are people who establish themselves before the age of forty using their inborn talents, but if they wish to maintain the wealth they have obtained, a perilous precipice will unfold dangerously from that moment till the day they die. This is because if they lack experience, the success they have achieved will culminate in pride or overconfidence. Success that comes too soon is poison.

Humankind balances experience with knowledge only after the age of forty. We can withstand the additional trouble of any upheavals in life only after we have lived the first half of our lives. It is only then that we don't waver, and realise what we are good and bad at.

Therefore, I think that business is a real game that always begins after forty. We can stand on our feet again, no matter what we did and how we floundered before the age of forty. As long as we are healthy. But there is a way to rise again even if our body has been hurt. Our body and mind share the same root in the real world. If we lack the energy to rise again because of poor health, our mind is rekindled when we begin to consistently take walks and do push-ups. We will surely succeed when we start anew with all the experience we have gained in forty years. The only fortune we can take with us to the day we die is what we have earned after the age of forty. No matter how much we earned before forty, only what we have earned after that will ultimately stay with us. We can therefore be reborn as outstanding entrepreneurs if we aren't afraid of the failures that transpired before we were forty, are cautious not to repeat the same mistakes, and cherish the experiences we amassed before forty.

68

The Courage to Admit Ignorance

We believe that professionals such as lawyers, doctors and university professors are wiser than ordinary people. We surmise that high-ranking politicians and successful businesspeople are also different from ordinary people in every respect. This is because we highly rate the process by which a person has strived to secure a professional job, or the fact that they have exerted themselves to join a high-ranking profession. We are therefore unable to dismiss their views, and we even solicit their opinions or agreement concerning issues that are beyond their professional areas.

There is no guarantee that doctors are better at finding their way or bringing up their children. Professors aren't more capable of making financial judgements, nor are they more knowledgeable about travelling in Europe. I have also seen people ask a pastor about investing or starting a new business. If that pastor had excelled in such entrepreneurial decisions, he would have gone into business and not pastoral work. He would have been commended a hundred times by his wife for going into business instead of serving in a church crowded with mothers-in-law, on a meagre pay with no guarantee for the future. Lawyers aren't more capable of philosophical thinking; and it's a fact that we are more trusting of high-ranking politicians' book publishing expertise because of the influence of their status, although there is absolutely no reason for them to receive more attention than the book publishing experiences of bankers.

Even in the office, subordinates solicit their superiors' opinions about matters outside work. Superiors feel pressured, as if they ought to respond to questions outside the scope of work. The person who is asking throws out all sorts of questions, and the one who is responding thoughtlessly answers even questions about which they are ignorant. This is because superiors believe there should be nothing that they are ignorant of. But it doesn't diminish a leader's prestige to admit ignorance about the things they are ignorant of. The biggest blow to a leader's prestige is when it becomes known that they don't know something after they have feigned knowledge about it. It's a shortcoming not to know something that is worth knowing. But it isn't a shortcoming not to know something that isn't worth knowing. Moreover, it's an enormous merit to admit ignorance about something we don't know. There are countless things that have gone wrong after we have feigned knowledge about things we don't know.

In other countries, the biggest villain – after a thief – is someone who leads others on the wrong path because they won't admit their ignorance but feign knowledge about something they don't know. The amount of time and money that has been squandered because of mistakes made when superiors feign knowledge about work or projects they are ignorant of is incalculable. Please admit ignorance if you don't know something, and seek the opinion of someone who does. If you are someone who has wasted several hours and even lost your car after someone has led you by the hand and shown you a path that they didn't really know, you will understand how hard it is on others when we pretend to know something we don't. If you don't know something, just say so.

69

Statistics Are Lies

Whenever I wait in line at an airport gate, it seems there are always problems with my queue. All the other queues move forward smoothly, but my queue gets held up, and there is absolutely no sign of it shortening. It isn't just on one occasion; it seems to happen every single time. It's the same at supermarkets, and even when I wait for buses.

The truth is it's fair for everyone, but among all our experiences our mind simply recalls far more memories of being treated unfairly. We often think we are unfortunate because our memories of easy solutions fade, and all we can remember are the terrible experiences.

There are three common lies in the world. Lies, damned lies and statistics. Statistics are lies disguised as maths. Statistics are concocted without consideration for actual information. We can concoct facts, just as I often recall myself as an unfortunate person when I'm queueing. All the graphs published in newspapers can convey very different messages, depending on their type and size. A twofold difference can be made to resemble a fourfold one using the height or breadth of bar graphs, and a ten percent difference can easily be made to look like fifty percent by removing the middle section of a bar. All the graphs that appear in newspapers have this hidden agenda. The word 'average' is also used to protect or dismiss people who are positioned outside the two extreme opposite ends of a statistic.

The average income of students who graduated from a university electronics department in 1994 is $100,000. But the average income will add up to $100,000 even if one or two graduates are earning $100 million while ninety percent of the cohort isn't even making $20,000. If I heard only that the average temperature was eighteen degrees, and then prepared for a camping trip and went into the desert, it would be insanely hot during the day, and I might freeze to death during the night.

Sample surveys are the most apt tool for deception. A sample survey that visited ten households in a neighbourhood of fifty thousand people and found that there were pianos in five households would be akin to saying that there were twenty five thousand pianos in the neighbourhood. Similarly, medical products, beauty products and health products use extremely small sample surveys to boast that sixty percent of users have seen results.

There are also occasions when lies are concocted by simply parading numbers. It seems more credible when one indicates that 34.17 percent, rather than one in three users, have seen results. It appears more realistic to report that 211,264 rather than 200,000 people have died in an earthquake; however, it's impossible to produce specific numbers beyond the sixth casualty in such a major incident. Such precise numbers are purely an intentional concoction, or a means to obtain trust. Colouring maps is also one of the classic techniques. There is a map of the United States in my office. I have coloured the states where we have opened at least one store. When we view it purely as a map, it looks as if Wyoming, where there is only one store, is on a par with Colorado, where there are dozens of stores.

If we wish to locate the loopholes in these statistics and not be fooled by them, we must ask who created them, what methods were used to carry out the study, and whether any data has been deliberately removed or added. And above all, we must be wary of people who foolishly and thoughtlessly use such data as the basis of their views.

270 · *Grab and Go*

Erroneous information produces erroneous judgements, and erroneous judgements produce lives that go awry. Conversely, if we can discern such information, we might not be fooled and can use a situation in a contrary way. We must always question statistics and strive to grasp the true intention behind them.

Bibliography

Corley, Thomas. *Rich Habits: The Daily Success Habits of Wealthy Individuals.* Minneapolis: Langdon Street Press, 2010.

Kim, Seung-Ho. *Jagigyeongyeong noteul* [Note on Self-Management]. Seoul: Hwanggeumsaja, 2009.

Kim, Seung-Ho. *Kimbap paneun CEO* [The Kimbap CEO]. Seoul: Hwanggeumsaja, 2015.

Epilogue

As it happened, I was flustered when Harriett Press proposed that we title this English edition *Grab and Go*. This was because these words were an official marketing phrase I had used when my business was expanding.

I didn't write this book to give an account of my business, and I was disappointed because this title might not properly convey what I wished to convey to Harriett Press's editor or readers. However, when I understood *Grab and Go* as an idiomatic English phrase, as the editor explained, I thought that to 'grab and go' with what we want in our life – which we live only once – could be a truly significant life goal.

I am one of those people who believe that anyone can achieve what they want through their own thoughts. Imagine a market filled with your dreams. And it's a world you can enter and grab all the many things you desire. The truth is: you can decide whether to set foot in this world. Whatever it is, you can grab and go with it. I hope this book will be a tool you can use to grab and go with what you truly want in life.

HARRIETT PRESS

Bridging Cultures with Stories

Harriett Press is a translation publisher founded in Singapore in 2018. We are on a mission to publish high-quality English translations of relevant, inspirational and influential Asian literature, and to make them accessible to English-speaking readers worldwide. We are constantly searching for distinctive voices and stories that will uplift, challenge and empower readers. We combine exceptional literary standards with artistic designs to enrich the experience of reading books in translation.

Follow us to stay updated on our latest news and newest titles:

harriettpress.com

facebook.com/sgharriettpress

instagram.com/harriettpress